Creating Great Web Graphics

Laurie McCanna

MIS:
PRESS

First Edition—1996

McCanna, Laurie.
    Creating great Web graphics / by Laurie McCanna.
       p. cm.
    ISBN 1-55828-479-6
     1. World Wide Web (Information retrieval system) 2. Computer graphics. I. Title.
    TK5105.888.M37 1996
    006.6'869--dc20   95-51547
                                          CIP

Printed in the United States of America.

10 9 8 7 6 5 4 3 2 1

Associate Publisher: Paul Farrell

Managing Editor: Cary Sullivan

Editor: Debra Williams Cauley

Copy Edit Manager: Shari Chappell

Design and Production: Joe McPartland

Technical Editor: Justin Powell

Copy Editor: Susan Ingrao

DEDICATION

For Tim, Adrian and Teague

CONTENTS

PART 2: INTERMEDIATE WEB GRAPHICS

PART 3: ADVANCED WEB TOPICS

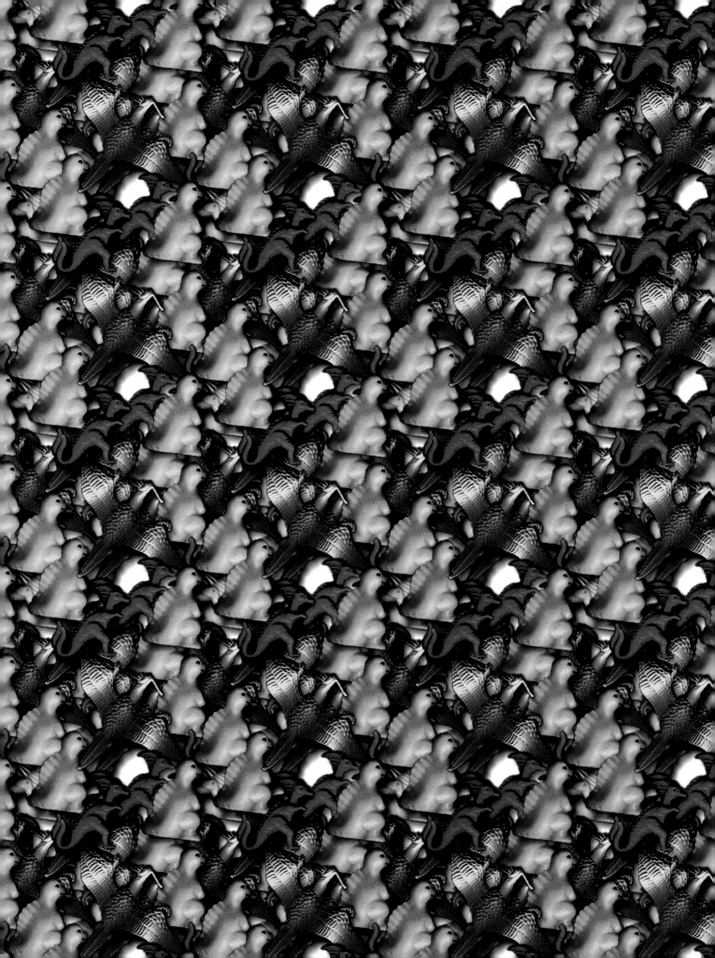

INTRODUCTION

Creating Great Web Graphics will help you to create professional-looking graphics, even if you don't have an artistic bone in your body. With instruction, anyone can create good-looking text with a drop shadow or a colored ball icon. Recipes for icons, page backgrounds, unusual edges, and type are accompanied by valuble advice and tricks to help you create cool graphics that load quickly. If you are graphically gifted, this book will inspire you to create even more imaginative and wonderful artwork for your website.

Each chapter tackles a specific topic and gives a step-by-step demonstration in both Photoshop version 3.0 for Windows (or higher) and Corel PhotoPaint version 6 for Windows. Photoshop is the standard tool for creating bitmapped graphics and Corel PhotoPaint, in its most recent revision, is a close cousin of Photoshop.

In addition to learning basic computer graphics techniques, such as how to create a drop shadow or 3D beveled icon, I'll discuss techniques for making graphics look great at low resolution. Another big issue for web design is creating graphics files that are small and therefore load quickly for the visitor to your website.

It's important to remember that the web has more in common with fast-paced television than it does with traditional paper printing. You may create beautiful graphics, but if the file sizes are too large, no one will stay at your website long enough to see your artwork since it will take so long to download. Creating fast loading, great-looking graphics is a good way to immediately engage the visitor to your website.

Before you jump into creating great web graphics, I will take a step back and examine how graphics fit into a web page.

ANATOMY OF A WEB PAGE

The software application used to view web pages is called a *browser*. Throughout the book I have used the most popular browser, Netscape. However, some online services (America Online, Netcom, CompuServe) have created their own browsers. One of the most challenging thing about creating web graphics is that each browser views the web page differently.

Graphics are used in a number of ways on a web page. In Figure I.1, the words "Adrian's Amazing Bean Dip" are actually a graphic. The blue lines behind the text are created by using a graphic that repeats or *tiles* over the background. The small, square icons next to the list of ingredients could be used as navigational devices. For example, when you click on the icon next to the "One big can of refried beans," the click would lead you to a second page with a picture of a big can of beans or more text. The icon could also just simply be used as graphic page decoration.

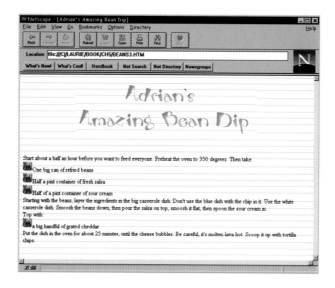

Figure I.1 A basic web page.

Web pages are created with *Hyper Text Markup Language (HTML)*. Using HTML, you can create backgrounds for your page, place images anywhere on your page, or (new, and not yet supported by all browsers) create banner elements that remain on the screen even when a reader scrolls past them. The graphic codes for HTML are some of the fastest-changing parts of the web specifications. See Appendix B for a current list of the tags that you can use with graphics.

Since HTML is a cross-platform language, you can create an HTML page with the same codes for viewing by Unix, Mac, or PC users. An HTML page can be created in a WYSIWYG HTML Editor software application, or, if you learn the HTML codes, you can simply create your entire web page in a word processor.

With HTML, each page element is placed on the page with an HTML code. For example, the graphic in Figure I.1 that reads "Adrian's Amazing Bean Dip" is named linehead.gif. It's inserted into the web page with the HTML code <img src="linehead.gif">. Spacing and alignment of web page elements are also controlled with HTML.

You can find out more about HTML by reading books such as *Teach Yourself Web Publishing In a Week* by Laura LeMay, or the *World Wide Web Bible* by Bryan Pfaffenberger.

One final warning about the Internet-technical side of web graphics—always remember that graphics files in whatever format are binary files, never text files. This can be important when you transfer files from your computer to the Internet (usually by FTP). If your graphics come out strange or won't show up at all, you may have let the computer transfer them as text files, which can corrupt your graphics and produce all kinds of problems.

GETTING STARTED

Before you begin the projects in this book, you should be familiar enough with your paint program to perform a few very basic tasks, including how to set the foreground and background colors for an image, how to use the Selection tool, and how to save a file.

Photoshop comes with very well written documentation. In addition, Photoshop has a very useful and well-written online **Help** function. You can access the **Help** function from the menu bar within Photoshop, as shown in Figure I.2.

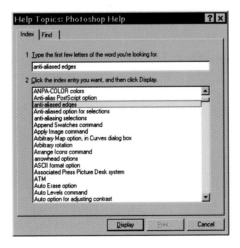

Figure I.2 Using Photoshop's **Help** function.

Corel has integrated the use of the right mouse button into version 6. In PhotoPaint, a good way to get an overview of any tool is to double-click on the tool. This will bring up the Tool Settings roll-up.

Using the right mouse button, right double-click on anything within the Tool Settings roll-up to receive more information. In Figure I.3, the word "Feather" was right double-clicked.

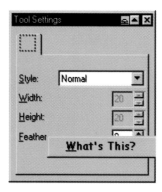

Figure I.3 Using the right mouse button in PhotoPaint.

In addition, there is an extensive online **Help** function within PhotoPaint. You can access the **Help** function from the menu bar within PhotoPaint (see Figure I.4).

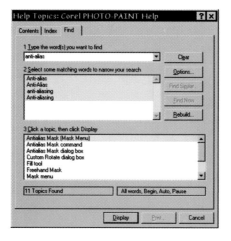

Figure I.4 Using PhotoPaint's **Help** function.

If you are a beginning user of Photoshop or PhotoPaint, I suggest that you work your way through the tutorials in this book first, and then go back to try some of the recipe variations. By the time you finish, you should be comfortable with all of the basic tools in the paint package that you use. I hope that the recipes inspire you to experiment with the tools in your paint program. A wonderful thing about working on the computer is that there is rarely only one way to achieve an effect.

For experienced Photoshop or PhotoPaint users, I suggest that you read Chapter One for information on anti-aliasing and file saving information. You may want to work through the recipes in the following chapters, and read Chapters Five, Eight, and Ten through Twelve for more technical information on creating web graphics.

This book is organized into three main sections: Creating Simple Web Graphics, Intermediate Web Graphics, and Advanced Web Topics.

In Creating Simple Web Graphics, Chapters One through Four, you'll learn about anti-aliasing, creating a drop shadow, making colored ball and beveled-edged icons, and how to create seamless pattern tiles.

Chapter One discusses anti-aliasing, which helps to remove jagged edges and create smoothness in web graphics. Chapter Two is a step-by-step demonstration of how to create those ever-popular colored ball icons, followed by ten different variations in the Recipes section. Chapter Three explains two different methods of creating beveled-edged icons, again followed by ten variations. In Chapter Four, you will learn to create seamless pattern tiles to use as web page backgrounds, as shown in Figure I.5.

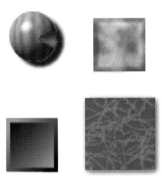

Figure I.5 Simple icons and a seamless background tile.

In the second section, Intermediate Web Graphics, (Chapters Five through Eight) you'll discover tips on designing web pages with color, how to fix a bad scan, how to create a hand-tinted photo, how to create interesting edges on images, and how to index colors.

I delve into using color and overall design techniques in Chapter Five, including how to troubleshoot a web page design. I also discuss several methods of finding the color hex code in Chapter Five. Scanning is a big issue, and Chapter Six discusses how to compensate, tweak, and correct bad scans. In addition Chapter Six discusses how to colorize a grayscale photograph, as shown in Figure I.6.

Figure 1.6 Colorizing a scanned photograph.

Adding creative edges on web graphics is a great way to add interest, and Chapter Seven gives ten methods to create interesting edges. Chapter Eight delves into some of the more important technical issues in designing for the web, including indexing, transparency, and a step-by-step guide for creating smaller graphics files.

In the final section of this book, Advanced Web Topics, you'll discover how to create text with a drop shadow (see Figure I.7), importing and exporting tips, how to speed up your work, and information on copyright and the web.

Figure I.7 Creating text effects.

Enlivening text with a glow or drop shadow is another great way to add some zip to a web page. Chapter Nine gives ten examples of type treatments. It's rare to work with files in one format, and Chapter Ten discusses importing and exporting files. Everybody hates drudgery, and Chapter Eleven gives tips for speeding up repetitive work. Chapter Twelve discusses copyright and the web, an important topic whether you are creating original work or planning on using clip art that someone else has created.

PART 1:
CREATING
SIMPLE
WEB
GRAPHICS

The Importance of Being Anti-Aliased, or Why Being Fuzzy is Sharp

Anti-aliasing has nothing to do with using the name of your mother's sister during the commission of a crime. (Ouch.) Actually, *anti-aliasing* is the most important tool in creating low-resolution graphics. It makes the stair-stepping, or "jaggies" of diagonal edges less apparent in graphics. Anti-aliasing creates a transition between two adjacent colors that appears as a slight blur. This blurring, conversely, makes the edges appear crisper.

Because anti-aliasing makes a smooth transition between colors, the edges appear cleaner and crisper. When you're working at screen resolution, you're using far fewer pixels, roughly only about a third of the pixels that you would if you were working at normal print resolution. Every pixel counts when you're working at a low resolution.

Anti-aliasing is especially helpful in increasing the legibility of type in graphics. In this chapter you'll work through two examples using anti-aliasing. The first example uses type, and the second example uses a simple graphic.

PHOTOSHOP: GETTING ANTI-ALIASED

1 Open a new file by selecting **File** from the menu bar, then **New**. Select a width of **300** pixels and a height of **100** pixels. The paper color should be set to **white**, and the color mode should be set to **RGB**. RGB is the color model that monitors use. Most PC monitors display at 96 pixels per inch, so that's what you should use for resolution. This isn't terribly important, since Web graphics will automatically display at the resolution of the viewer's monitor. Creating images at a higher resolution will not make the images any clearer; it will only make them display larger.

All of the Photoshop examples in the book assume that you are using RGB mode, 96 pixels per inch, and the paper color set to white, unless otherwise noted.

If you're used to creating graphics for print, it might be useful to note that for web graphics, pixels per inch is equal to dots per inch, and that you won't want to use CMYK color. RGB color has a greater range than CMYK color and uses a similar color scheme to what your monitor normally does.

Choose **black** as your foreground color. (The type will be filled with the foreground color).

2 Select the **Type** tool, then click on your image. This will bring up the Type Tool dialog box. Make sure that the **anti-aliasing** checkbox is checked. Set the type size to about **20** points, and type out, **This is anti-aliased type**.

To reposition your type, you can move the cursor over the type until it changes into an arrow, and then drag the type into position. If you prefer, you can nudge the type into position one pixel at a time by using the arrow keys on your keyboard.

3 Select the **Type** tool, then click on your file. Type out **This is NOT anti-aliased type**. Be sure to deselect the **Anti-Aliasing** option, as shown in Figure 1.1.

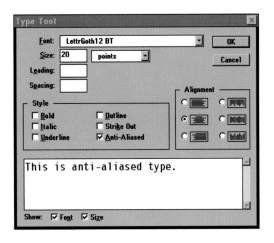

Figure 1.1 Using Photoshop's Help Function

4 Compare the two lines of type, as in Figure 1.2. See the difference a little anti-aliasing can make!

This is anti-aliased type.

This is NOT anti-aliased type.

Figure 1.2 Comparing anti-aliased and non anti-aliased type

PHOTOSHOP: ANTI-ALIASING OTHER TYPES OF GRAPHICS

Often, you'll be presented with a bitmapped image that looks great except for its offensively jagged edges. If you need to anti-alias an entire image, your best bet is to resize the image using the **Image/Image Size** option. When Photoshop resizes an image, it automatically anti-aliases the edges for you. I'll discuss anti-aliasing imported files more in Chapter Ten.

Many of the tools within Photoshop are automatically anti-aliased as well, including the paintbrush, airbrush, and blur tools from the Tool palette. There may be a checkbox on the Options palette that turns the anti-aliasing on or off for that particular tool.

And for those little touch-ups, I've found the Smudge tool in Photoshop to be perfect.

1. Start with a new file 100x100 pixels. Double-click on the **Pencil** tool to open the Options/Brushes palette. Set the brush size to the smallest size (1 pixel) and draw a red triangle by holding down the **Shift** key and clicking in three places. You can fill the triangle with red if you like, as shown in Figure 1.3.

Figure 1.3 Right side of triangle has been anti-aliased

2. Select the **Smudge** tool. Set 50% pressure in the Options palette, and select a small brush size. Holding down the **Shift** key, Shift-click at two points on the triangle, across a jagged edge. In Figure 1.3, the right edge of the triangle has been anti-aliased.

PHOTOPAINT: GETTING ANTI-ALIASED

1 Open a new file by selecting **File** from the menu bar, then **New**. Set the paper color to **white**. The Image Size should be set to **Custom** and a width of **300** pixels and a height of **100** pixels. The default color mode in PhotoPaint is 24-Bit RGB, the color model that monitors use. Most PC monitors display at 96 pixels per inch, so that's what you should use for Resolution setting.

All of the PhotoPaint examples in the book assume that you are using 24-Bit RGB color, 96 pixels per inch, and the paper color white unless otherwise noted.

If you're accustomed to creating graphics for print that you won't want to use CMYK color. RGB color has a greater range than CMYK color.

Select **black** as your paint color. The paint color is the color the type will be filled with. You can select the fill color by right-clicking on the palette at the bottom of the screen.

2 Double-click on the **Type** tool. This will bring up the Tool Settings dialog box, as shown in Figure 1.4. Make sure that the **anti-aliasing** checkbox is checked. Set the type size to about **20** points, click on your file, and type out, **This is anti-aliased type**. If you need to reposition your type, you can drag the type into position.

Figure 1.4 PhotoPaint's Tool Settings roll-up

3 Click on your file with the **Type** tool. Type out **This is NOT anti-aliased type.** Deselect the **Anti-Aliasing** option.

4 Compare the two lines of type as shown in Figure 1.5. You can see how anti-aliasing creates more legible type. If you want to save this file, you'll need to apply **Objects/Combine/All Objects** with **Background** first.

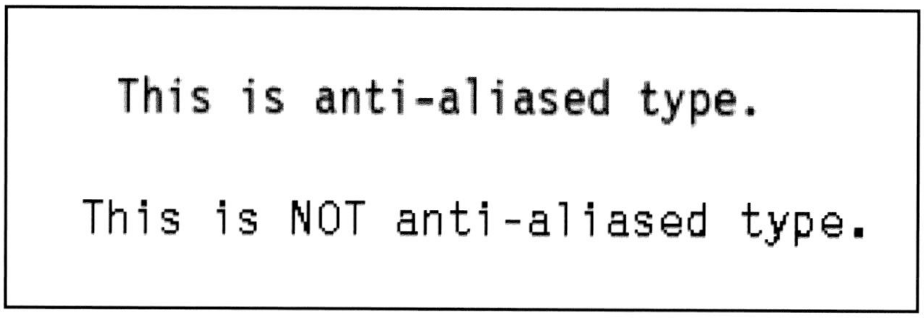

This is anti-aliased type.

This is NOT anti-aliased type.

Figure 1.5 Comparing anti-aliased and non anti-aliased type

PHOTOPAINT: ANTI-ALIASING OTHER TYPES OF GRAPHICS

If you need to anti-alias an entire bitmap image, your best bet is to resize the image using the **Image/Resample** with the **Process** set to **Anti-Aliased**. PhotoPaint has introduced the option of resampling a bitmapped file when you open it, but this does not anti-alias the image when it resamples. It's best to open the file, then use **Image/Resample**.

I'll discuss anti-aliasing imported files, including CorelDRAW files, in Chapter Ten.

Many of the tools within PhotoPaint are automatically anti-aliased. In the Tool Settings palette (shown in Figure 1.6), if you indicate an amount in the Soft Edge box, the Brush tool will be anti-aliased.

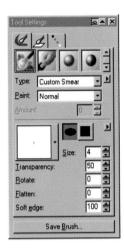

Figure 1.6 Tool Settings roll-up for the smear brush

If you've created a mask and want the edges of the mask to be anti-aliased, you'll want to use the checkbox on the Mask roll-up, with the amount set to **1** or **2** pixels.

And for those little touch-ups, I've found the Smear tool in PhotoPaint to be the best answer.

1 Start with a file 100x100 pixels. Double-click on the **Straight Line** tool to open the Tool Settings roll-up. Set the size to **1** pixel. Use the Straight Line tool to draw a red triangle by clicking in three places. Double-click to finish the triangle. You can fill the triangle with red if you like.

2 Double-click on the **Effects** tool, which will bring up the Tool Settings roll-up. **Select Size, 4**; **Transparency, 50**; **Rotate, 0**; **Flatten, 0**; and **Soft Edge, 50**. Hold down the **Alt** key, and **Alt+click** the **Smear** tool on two points of the triangle. This will connect the two clicks using the **Smear** tool. In Figure 1.7, I've anti-aliased the right edge of the triangle. You may want to save the variation of the **Smear** tool you've just created for future use.

Figure 1.7 Right side of the triangle has been anti-aliased

A NOTE ON SAVING FILES

I know you're probably eager to start getting your images up onto your website. The most commonly used file format for web graphics is the gif format. Gif files contain a maximum of 256 colors. Gif files are compressed, which means that they have smaller file sizes than uncompressed file formats.

I'll discuss the gif format and transparency further in Chapter Eight. But for now, here's how to save your image as a gif.

If you try to save your file as a gif when the file is still in RGB color, you'll notice that the gif file format is not even listed. You need to reduce the colors to 256 or less.

You can do this in Photoshop by using **Mode/Indexed** color. From there, you'll see that the number of colors are listed for your image. Normally, you'll want to select **8** bits (or less), **Adaptive Color**, and **Diffusion**. Once you have indexed the colors for the image, you can save the file in gif format.

To save your file as a gif in PhotoPaint, apply **Image/Convert to/256** colors. Select **Palette Type**, **Optimized**; **Dither Type**, **Error Diffusion**. For now, save the gif in 87a format.

Remember that gif is a lossy format, that is, you lose information from your image when you save it as a gif file. If you think you'll need to revise, resize, or print the artwork you create, you'll want to also save your file in a format that is not compressed, such as tif, or bmp. Also, once you have indexed the colors for an image, you won't be able to use filters on the image, or use brushes with anti-aliased edges. (Learn about indexing in Chapter 8.) If you've saved a file as .gif and want to use a filter on it, you'll need to convert the image back to RGB 24-bit color.

Saving as a gif is usually the very last step in creating web graphics.

This is also a good time to start thinking about naming conventions for your files. You'll want to use all lowercase letters when you name your files. Normally, in the DOS world, it doesn't matter if you use upper- or lowercase when naming files. UNIX, however, is case sensitive. If you name a file HySTErIA.GIF, and your HTML code indicates hysteria.gif, you could run into problems.

And yet another thing I've learned the hard way is that you shouldn't use symbols within a file name. I had gotten into the habit of naming files giggle#1.gif, giggle#2.gif, and so on. Using symbols in a file name can create problems when the files are copied over onto the UNIX server. My client couldn't view a gif I had created on the UNIX server until it had been renamed without the number sign.

Now you know what anti-aliasing is, you'll end up using it all the time. It's not exciting or glamorous, but using anti-aliasing within images and especially with type will make your images appear cleaner and more professional.

Chapter **2**

MAKING THOSE CLEVER LITTLE COLORED BALL ICONS

You've seen these friendly little icons on web pages all over the place. I consider these colored ball icons to be the Smiley Face (remember have a nice day?) of the '90s. No matter how you feel about these icons, creating them can be a great way to learn some of the basic tools in Photoshop and PhotoPaint.

I'll show you two basic ways to craft these clever dollops of artwork, and I'll provide recipes for variations of the colored ball icon. The first method uses traditional painting tools, including the fill and airbrush tools. The second method (for those of you who don't want to get your hands dirty) is done entirely with filters.

Just a couple of quick notes about working at screen (monitor) resolution. You'll notice that I'm working with the images at a pixel level. In the screen shots, you'll also notice that I've used the rulers, set to pixels, to help orient you to how small I'm actually working. You'll find it helpful to change your units of measurement within the paint program you're using from inches to pixels. You can do this in Photoshop by going to **File/Preferences/Units/Ruler Units** or in PhotoPaint by going to **Tools/Options/General** and changing the units to **pixels**. If you think it would be helpful to use the rulers, simply use **Ctrl+R** to view them.

It would be overkill and a waste of time to work this close up for images that would be printed at 300 dpi or higher, but you do need to work at a zoomed-in rate much of the time for work that will be displayed at 96 dpi or less.

Another thing to be aware of as you begin to experiment is that some of the tools in the paint programs are tweaked for use at higher resolutions. For example, you'll notice that using some filters (such as the Color Halftone, Mezzotint or Wind filters in Photoshop) will obliterate a file at 96 dpi.

Now, on with the show.

PHOTOSHOP: COLORED BALLS WITHOUT FILTERS

1 Open a small file in Photoshop, 40x40 pixels at 96 dpi. Use the selection tool to draw a circle (the tool in the top upper left of the toolbox). The selection tool should be set to **Elliptical**, as shown in Figure 2.1. If your toolbox shows a rectangular selection, double-click on the **selection** tool. This will bring up the Option palette for the selection tool, and you can change the setting from Rectangular to **Elliptical**. Recalling the lesson on anti-aliasing from the Chapter One, (you do remember, don't you?), check the **anti-aliasing** checkbox so that the icon will have an anti-aliased edge.

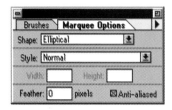

Figure 2.1 Options for the selection tool

Hold down the **Shift** key while you're creating the selection to constrain the ellipse to a circle. Leave some room to include a drop shadow as shown in Figure 2.2.

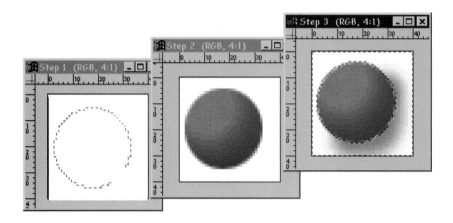

Figure 2.2 Creating a colored ball icon

Make sure that red is showing as your foreground color and gray as the background color. Double-click on the **Gradient** tool to open its Option palette.

Check the Option palette for the Gradient Tool. It should be set to **Normal** and **Radial** as shown in Figure 2.3.

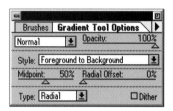

Figure 2.3 Gradient tool options

Drag the Gradient tool from the upper-left corner to the lower-right corner of the circle to fill the selection with a smooth gradation.

 From the menu bar, apply **Select/Inverse**. This will mask out the circle, allowing you to paint a drop shadow behind the circle. Use the **Airbrush** tool and dark gray as the color, to paint a drop shadow along the edge of the circle.

For the finishing touch, apply **Select/None** (or **Ctrl+D**) and change the foreground color to white. Add a small highlight using the Airbrush tool on the upper-right area of the ball, as shown in Figure 2.4.

Figure 2.4 The finished icon

PHOTOSHOP: COLORED BALLS USING FILTERS

This method of creating a colored ball icon requires both the Alien Skin Drop Shadow filter and the Glass Lens filter from Kai's Power Tools.

The Glass Lens Filter is part of the Kai's Power Tool package, a set of useful filters created by HSC Software. The Drop Shadow filter is part of Alien Skin Software's set of filters called the Black Box.

1 As in the first example, open a small file in Photoshop, 40 pixels by 40 pixels, or use **Ctrl+N**. Use the selection tool set to **ellipse** to create a circular selection, as shown in Figure 2.5.

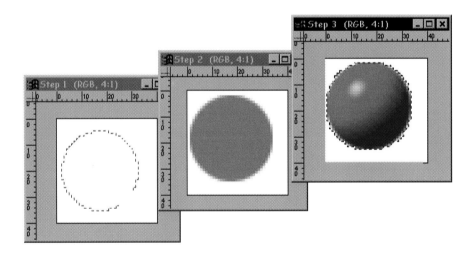

Figure 2.5 Creating a colored ball icon using filters

2 Use the Fill tool to fill the selection with red.

3 From the menu bar, apply **Filter/KPT/Glass Lens Bright**.

4 From the menu bar, apply **Filter/Alien Skin/Drop Shadow** filter to finish off your creation, setting the shadow offset amount to about **4** pixels for the horizontal and vertical offset measurements. Select **black** as the shadow color. You've used the Drop Shadow after the Glass Lens Bright filter because using the Drop Shadow removes the selection from your image, shown in Figure 2.6.

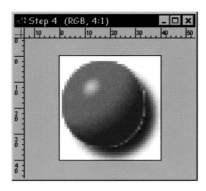

Figure 2.6 The finished icon created with filters

PHOTOPAINT: COLORED BALL ICONS WITHOUT FILTERS

One of the differences between Corel PhotoPaint and Photoshop is terminology. What PhotoPaint calls a *mask* roughly equates to what Photoshop calls a *selection*. It's easy to become confused and frustrated trying to use a mask (or selection) tool. Masks and selections are really more equivalent to the kinds of tools photographers use than the kind of tools artists traditionally use. A mask or selection can be as simple as a geometric shape (say, a circle) that allows you to paint within a circle. A mask or selection can be as complex and as powerful as applying an filter using a grayscale photo to mask the image.

I'm going to start slow and sneak up on some of these masking tools. No excuses, no notes from home. You're going to jump right into PhotoPaint and create some of those timeless, eternal little round ball icons using the masking tools.

1 Open a small file, 40 pixels by 40 pixels, at 96 dpi.

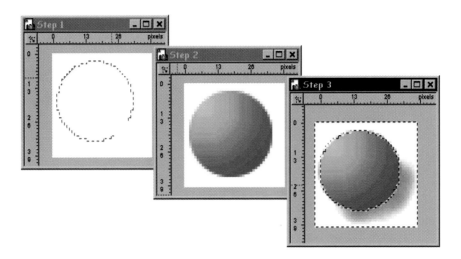

Figure 2.7 Creating a colored ball icon

2 Double-click on the **Circle Mask** tool (shown in Figure 2.8) to open the Tool Settings roll-up. Recalling the previous chapter, check the **anti-alias** checkbox. Hold down the **Control** key while you're creating the mask to constrain the ellipse to a circle. Make the circle a little smaller than the total image area so that you have room for the drop shadow.

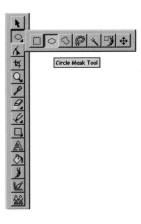

Figure 2.8 The circle mask tool in PhotoPaint

3 Next, double-click on the **Fill** tool to open the Tool Settings roll-up. Select the **Fountain Fill** icon, and select **Edit**. You will want to select Type: **Radial**; Center Offset—Horizontal: **-26**, Vertical: **26**; **Two Color Blend**; From: **dark blue**; To: **light blue**. Fill the mask.

4 From the menu bar, select **Mask/Invert** to allow you to paint next to but not on the ball. Select the **Paintbrush** tool, double-click to open the Tool Settings roll-up. Select the **Airbrush** to paint a soft gray shadow. Select **Mask/None**. Change the foreground color to **white** and use the Airbrush to paint a highlight on the upper-left side of the ball (as shown in Figure 2.9).

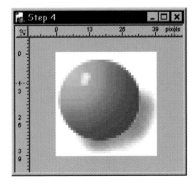

Figure 2.9 The finished icon

PHOTOPAINT: CREATING COLORED BALLS USING FILTERS

This method of creating a colored ball icon requires both the Alien Skin Drop Shadow filter and the Glass Lens filter from Kai's Power Tools.

The Glass Lens Filter is part of the Kai's Power Tool package, a set of useful filters created by HSC Software. The Drop Shadow filter is part of Alien Skin Software's set of filters called the Black Box.

The following first two steps are identical to the way you started to create the ball icon in the preceding example with PhotoPaint.

1 Open a small file, 40 pixels by 40 pixels, at 96 dpi. Use the Circle Masking tool. Hold down the **Control** key while you're creating the Mask to constrain the ellipse to a circle. Make the circle a little smaller than the image so you have room for the drop shadow, shown in Figure 2.10.

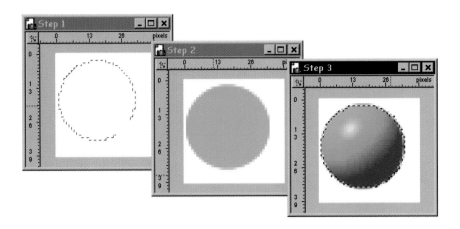

Figure 2.10 Creating a colored ball icon using filters

2 Select the **Fill** tool. Double-click the **Fill** tool to open the Tool Settings roll-up, click on **Uniform** Fill, and choose a **light blue** or select a light blue from the color palette at the bottom of the screen using the right mouse button. Fill the mask.

3 Apply **Effects/KPT/Glass Lens Bright Filter**.

4 Finally, apply the **Effects/Alien Skin/Drop Shadow** filter, using **4** pixels for both the X and Y offset measurements. Select **black** as the shadow color. The finished icon is shown in Figure 2.11.

Figure 2.11 The finished icon created with filters

RECIPES FOR COLORED BALL ICONS CREATED IN PHOTOSHOP

Note: All of the following files below were begun with a file 40x40 pixels, RGB, 96 dpi, and a circular selection with room for a drop shadow.

Fill selection with yellow. Apply **Filter/KPT 2.0 Filters/Glass Lens Bright**. Apply **Filter/Alien Skin/Drop Shadow** with X and Y offsets set at **4**, blur at **3** pixels, opacity **80**, and Shadow color to **black**. Use the paintbrush set to **1** or **2** pixels with **black** color to draw the face. Change the color to **white** and paint the highlights on the eyes. Have a nice day!

Fill selection with blue. Apply **Filter/Noise/Add Noise** filter with Amount set at **70** and Distribution set to **Gaussian**. Apply **Filter/KPT 2.0 Filters/Glass Lens Bright**, followed by **Filter/Alien Skin/Drop Shadow** with the same settings as before.

Fill selection with a very light gray. Apply **Filter/ KPT 2.0 Filters/Glass Lens Bright**, followed by **Filter/Alien Skin/Drop Shadow** with the same settings as before. Make a smaller elliptical selection and fill it with dark blue. Make another elliptical selection (either draw it or use **Select/Modify/Contract/3 pixels**) and fill with black. Apply **Filter/ KPT 2.0 Filters/Glass Lens Bright** to the black circle.

Fill selection with blue. Apply **Filter/Noise/Add Noise**, followed by **Filter/Noise/Dust & Scratches** with a radius of **1** pixel. To finish, apply **Filter/KPT 2.0 Filters/Glass Lens Bright**, followed by **Filter/Alien Skin/Drop Shadow** with the same settings as before.

Fill selection with a light green, then draw dark green vertical stripes with the Paintbrush tool. Apply **Filter/KPT 2.0 Filters/Glass Lens Bright**, followed by **Filters/Alien Skin/Drop Shadow** using the same settings as before. Use the **Lasso Selection** tool to draw a triangle on the right side of the circle. Set the foreground color to **magenta** and the background color to **red**. Apply the **Gradient** tool from the top of the triangle to the bottom of the triangle.

Fill selection with blue. **Apply Filter/KPT 2.0 Filters/Glass Lens Bright** twice. Apply **Filter/Alien Skin/Drop Shadow**. Make a smaller circle selection inside the first circle and apply **Filter/KPT 2.0 Filters/Glass Lens Bright**. Apply **Image/Rotate/90° CCW**.

Fill selection with magenta. Apply **Filter/KPT 2.0 Filters/Glass Lens Bright** and **Filter/Alien Skin/Drop Shadow**. Change the foreground color to black, and use the Type tool to create the question mark.

Fill selection with light blue. Apply **Filter/Pixelate/Color Halftone** with the default settings except for the Radius set to **4** pixels. Apply **Filter/KPT 2.0 Filters/Glass Lens Bright** and **Filter/Alien Skin/Drop Shadow** filters.

Fill the selection with red. Paint yellow vertical stripes using the **Paintbrush** tool. Apply **Filter/Distort/Ripple** with Setting: **Small**; Amount: **-200**. Apply **Filter/KPT 2.0 Filters/Glass Lens Bright** and **Filter/Alien Skin/Drop Shadow** filters.

Fill the selection with yellow. Paint green vertical stripes using the Paintbrush tool. Apply **Filter/Distort/Twirl** with Amount: **600**. Apply **Filter/KPT 2.0 Filters/Glass Lens Bright** and **Filter/Alien Skin/Drop Shadow** filters.

RECIPES FOR COLORED BALL ICONS CREATED WITH PHOTOPAINT

Note: All of the following files were begun with a file 40x40 pixels, 24-bit color, 96 dpi, and a circular mask with room for a drop shadow. Remember to anti-alias the mask by checking the **anti-aliasing** checkbox on the Tool Settings roll-up for the mask.

Fill mask with purple using **Uniform** fill. Set the foreground color to **light blue**. Double-click on the **Paintbrush** tool. If you select the brush sample, you will be able to scroll through a group of brush patterns. Select a pattern to your liking and apply to the mask. Apply the **Effects/KPT 2.0 Filters/Glass Lens Bright** filter, followed by the **Effects/Alien Skin/Drop Shadow** filter with X and Y shadows offset to **4** pixels, Blur set to **3** pixels, Opacity set to **80%** and Shadow color set to **black**.

Fill mask with yellow. Apply the **Effects/KPT 2.0 Filters/Glass Lens Bright** filter. Set the foreground color to **purple**. Apply **Effects/Alien Skin/Drop Shadow** filter with X and Y shadows offset to **0** pixels, Blur set to **4** pixels, Opacity set to **100%**, and Shadow color set to **foreground**.

Fill mask with gray. Apply the **Effects/KPT 2.0 Filters/Glass Lens Soft** filter. Use the **Line** tool to draw a dark gray vertical line and a white vertical line. Apply **Effects/Alien Skin/Drop Shadow** with X and Y shadows offset to **4** pixels, Blur set to **3** pixels, Opacity to **80%**, and Shadow color to **black**. Draw another dark gray vertical line to finish.

Double-click on the **Fill** tool, choose **Texture Fill**, click on **Edit**, and set to **Styles/Fiber**. Apply fill to mask. Apply the **Effects/KPT 2.0 Filters/Glass Lens Bright** and **Effects/Alien Skin/Drop Shadow** filters with the same settings as before.

PhotoPaint

Fill mask with magenta. Use **Eraser** tool to draw stripes on the circle. Apply **Effects/2D Effects/Swirl** filter set to **-270°**. Apply the **Effects/KPT 2.0 Filters/Glass Lens Bright** and **Effects/Alien Skin/Drop Shadow** filters with the same settings as before.

Fill mask with a cream color. Double-click on the **Paintbrush** tool. Set foreground color to **blue**. Choose the **Spraypaint** can, set to **Textured Spatter**, and apply to circle. Apply the **Effects/KPT 2.0 Filters/Glass Lens Bright** and **Effects/Alien Skin/Drop Shadow** filters with the same settings as before.

Fill mask with black. Apply the **Effects/KPT 2.0 Filters/Glass Lens Bright** and **Effects/Alien Skin/Drop Shadow** filters with the same settings as before. Make a white circular mask inside the ball. Apply the **Effects/KPT 2.0 Filters/Glass Lens Bright** filter. Add the number with the Text tool.

Fill mask with black. Apply the **Effects/KPT 2.0 Filters/Glass Lens Soft** filter. Apply **Effects/Alien Skin/Drop Shadow** filter with X Offset to **-4** and Y Offset to **-3**, Blur set to **3**, Opacity set to **20**.

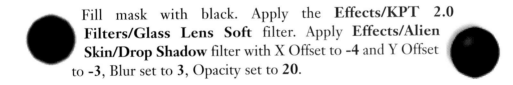

Fill mask with red. Apply the **Effects/KPT 2.0 Filters/Glass Lens Bright** filter. Apply **Mask/Shape/Reduce** set to **4** pixels and apply **Effect/KPT 2.0 Filters/Glass Lens Bright** again. Apply **Object/Create From Mask**. Apply **Object/Rotate/90° Counterclockwise**. Apply **Mask/Create from Object(s)**. Apply **Mask/Shape/Expand** set to **4** pixels. Apply the **Effects/Alien Skin/Drop Shadow** filter with the X and Y shadows set to **4**, Blur set to **3**, Opacity set to **80**, and the Shadow set to **black**. Use the Paintbrush to place 4 red dabs of paint, then 4 gray dabs of paint.

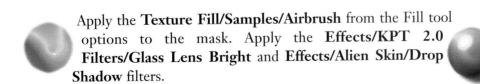

Apply the **Texture Fill/Samples/Airbrush** from the Fill tool options to the mask. Apply the **Effects/KPT 2.0 Filters/Glass Lens Bright** and **Effects/Alien Skin/Drop Shadow** filters.

PhotoPaint

Creating Icons with Beveled Edges, or Icon Designing Like a Pro

An icon on a web page can be used for navigation or a simple page decoration. However, the most important feature of a icon is clarity. If the person viewing the icon has to think about what the icon means, then it's a poorly designed icon. Thinking back over your experience of using software, I'm sure that you can remember at least a few frustrating experiences you've had with ambiguous icons.

Poor icon design is compounded by what I call "icon blindness." It seems as if each new revision of software adds another layer of icons to the toolbar. One morning I sat and counted how many icons I saw among the different applications that I use, including online services, word processing and paint programs. I stopped counting at 100, and I'm sure that's not unusual.

By the time the reader gets to your web page, they've been inundated with little tiny pictures. The visitor to your website doesn't want to figure out if the icon means reload, home, previous page, or don't forget to write home. Unlike most artwork, the point of icons is not to make the viewer think. The icon should have an immediate association for the viewer.

The alternatives to a picture-only icon are a picture combined with text, or an icon with text only. It is not a failure of design skills to use text on an icon.

Since I've created my share of icons for software running under Windows, I'd like to share a few insights about designing icons. For starters, if it takes more than three words to describe the purpose of the icon, there is rarely any way to condense the concept into a picture without text to support it. As an example, I was once asked to design an icon that would describe "sorting information by the information's past relationships to other information within a database."

For icons that are used as simple page decoration, in place of bullets, you should keep them simple. Remember that basic design principles apply not only to printed pages, but to web pages also. You want to use the artwork you are creating to guide the viewer's eye to the important points on the page.

One way to streamline work on a website is to decide ahead of time what size the graphics will be. If you keep a consistent size to the graphics at your website, it can help to organize and unify the design of each page. For instance, you might decide that all icons and icon bars will be 40 pixels in height, and all headers will be 500x100 pixels, etc.

To get a general idea of basic icon sizes, the Windows icons that reside on your desktop are usually 32x32 pixels. Toolbar icons that you see in applications like Word and Corel, are usually 24x24 pixels. If you plan on adding text or backgrounds or drop shadows to your icons, you'll probably want to work a little larger than 32x32 pixels.

In the following tutorials, you'll create two different types of icons. One will be a simple beveled icon with a picture, and the other will be an icon with a textured background and beveled edge and text. After the tutorial you'll find recipes for other three-dimensional icons.

PHOTOSHOP: CREATING A SIMPLE ICON

1 Open a new file, 40x40 pixels, 96 pixels/inch, RGB mode. Using the **Fill** tool, fill the image with light gray, as shown in Figure 3.1.

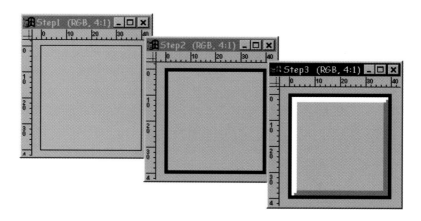

Figure 3.1 Creating a simple icon in Photoshop

2 Double-click on the **Pencil** tool to bring up the Options/Brushes dialog box. You'll want to select the smallest brush size (which is 1 pixel) and set the foreground color to **black**. Hold down the **Shift** key. This will constrain your drawing to a straight line. Draw a 1-pixel black line all the way around the outside edge of the image.

3 Change the foreground color to **dark gray**. Draw a 2-pixel wide dark gray line at the bottom and right edges. Change the foreground color to white. Draw a 2-pixel-wide **white** line at the top and left edges. The gray and white edges should meet at 45° angles.

4 Now draw the arrow. Draw the bottom edge of the arrow with a 1-pixel white line, as shown in Figure 3.2

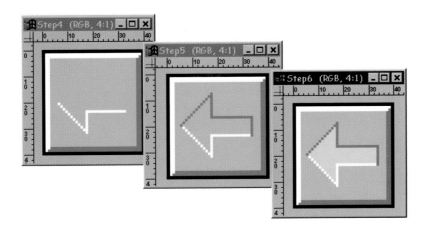

Figure 3.2 Adding an arrow to the icon

5 Draw the top portion of the arrow with a dark gray 1-pixel line.

6 Fill the arrow with a gray that's a little lighter than the gray you used to fill the icon. You have now designed your first icon, shown in Figure 3.3.

Figure 3.3 The finished icon

PHOTOSHOP: CREATING A TEXTURED ICON

1 Open a new file, 100 pixels wide by 40 pixels tall. Fill the image with light blue as shown in Figure 3.4.

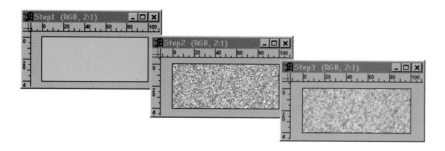

Figure 3.4 Creating a textured icon in Photoshop

2 Use the Filter/Noise/Add Noise filter at 130, and set the type to **Uniform**.

3 Apply **Filter/Blur/Blur**.

4 With the Pencil tool set to 1 pixel, draw a black line all the way around the image, as shown in Figure 3.5.

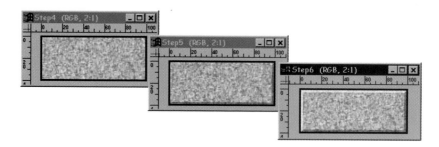

Figure 3.5 Adding a beveled edge

5 Double-click on the **Pencil** tool , which will open the Options/Brushes palette. Change the mode from Normal to **Multiply**, and change the Opacity to **70%**. This will allow some of the texture to show through the shadow you'll draw on the edge of the icon. Using a dark gray, draw a two pixel border at the bottom and right edges of the icon.

6 Change the foreground color to **white**, and set the Mode to **Screen** on the Options/Brushes palette. Leave the Opacity at **70%**, and draw a 2-pixel border at the top and left edges of the icon.

As a final step, add some text to your icon, as shown in Figure 3.6. Don't forget to anti-alias your text!

Figure 3.6 The finished icon with text

PHOTOSHOP AND THE ALIEN SKIN FILTERS

Alien Skin makes a set of filters called The Black Box that runs from within Photoshop, PhotoPaint, or Micrografx Picture Publisher. All of the filters are useful, but for making icons, the Outer Bevel filter works especially well. The Outer Bevel filter will add a shadow and a highlight to your image, giving it a 3D bevel in two steps.

Repeat steps 1–3 from the preceding textured icon project. With the rectangular selection tool, make a selection that is a little smaller than the entire image. Next, apply **Select/Feather** at **2** pixels. As the final step, apply **Filters/Alien Skin/Outer Bevel**, using the Typical preset. Your finished icon will look like Figure 3.7.

Figure 3.7 Using a filter to create an icon

PHOTOPAINT: CREATING A SIMPLE ICON

1 Start with a new file, using 24-bit color, a size of 40x40 pixels, and the DPI set to **96**. Fill the image with light gray as shown in Figure 3.8.

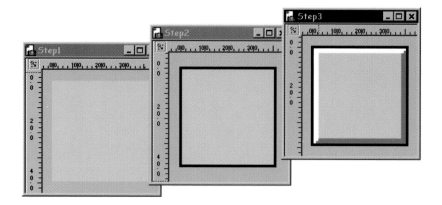

Figure 3.8 Creating a simple icon in PhotoPaint

2 Using the Straight Line tool set to **1** pixel, draw a black line around the outer edge of the image. You can constrain the Straight Line tool to a 90° angle by holding down the **Control** key while you click at the corners of the image. Double-click with the Straight Line tool to finish the black line.

3 Use the Straight Line tool to draw a 2-pixel-wide gray border at the bottom and left edges of the image. Draw a 2-pixel-wide white border at the top and left edges of the image.

4 With the Straight Line tool, draw a dark gray line as shown in Figure 3.9.

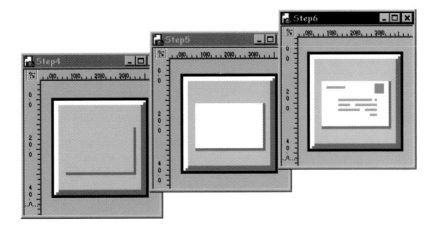

Figure 3.9 Adding a picture to the icon

5 Draw a white line to complete the rectangle, and fill with white.

6 Finish the envelope by drawing gray lines to simulate text and a blue square, shown in Figure 3.10.

Figure 3.10 The finished icon

PHOTOPAINT: CREATING A TEXTURED ICON

1 Start with a new file, using 24-bit color, a size of 100x40 pixels, and the DPI set to **96**. Fill the image with a cream color as shown in Figure 3.11.

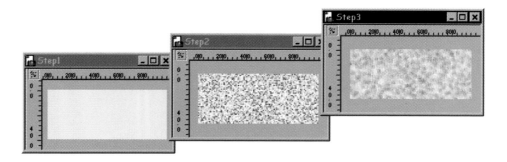

Figure 3.11 Creating a textured icon in PhotoPaint

2 Apply **Effects/Noise/Add Noise**, being sure to check the **color noise** checkbox. The Level should be set to **50**, the Density, **50**, and the Type, **Gaussian**.

3 Apply **Effect/Blur/Jaggy Despeckle**, using Width, **3**; Height, **3**.

4 Using the Straight Line tool, draw a 1-pixel black line around the outer edge of the image as shown in Figure 3.12.

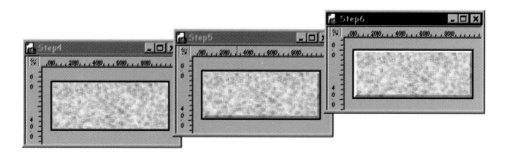

Figure 3.12 Adding a beveled edge

5 Set the Transparency for the Straight Line tool to **10**, and the Mode to **Multiply** to allow some of the texture to appear on the bevel. Draw a 2-pixel orange line at the bottom and right sides of the image.

Draw a 2-pixel white edge at the left and top of the image.

Add some text to the icon to finish. Don't forget to anti-alias your text! After you've used the text tool, apply **Object/Combine/All Objects with Background**. Your finished icon will look like Figure 3.13.

Figure 3.13 The finished icon with text

PHOTOPAINT AND ALIEN SKIN FILTERS

Several of the Alien Skin filters are built into PhotoPaint. You'll be using the filter named The Boss, which is especially useful for creating beveled edges. The Boss filter creates a shadow and a highlight on the image, giving it that three dimensional look.

Repeat steps 1–3 to create the textured icon. Then apply **Mask/All**, **Mask/Feather at Width**, **2 pixels**; **Direction**, **Inside**; and **Edges, Soft**. Apply **Effects/3D/The Boss**, using the Default setting. The finished icon will look like Figure 3.14.

Figure 3.14 Using a filter to create an icon

By varying the size and position (inside or outside) for the feather on the mask, you can vary the size of the bevel on the icon.

RECIPES FOR ICONS IN PHOTOSHOP

Start with an image 40x40 pixels. Fill the image with light gray, draw a 1-pixel black line around the outer edge. Make a 2-pixel dark gray edge at the top and left sides of the image. On the bottom and right edges, draw a 2-pixel white edge. This type of shadowing on an icon is generally used to indicate a depressed, or "clicked" position for the icon.

Start with a new file, 100x40 pixels. Make an elliptical selection, and Select/Feather by 1 pixel. Fill the selection with a light blue, and apply **Filter/KPT Filter/Glass Lens Soft**.

Start with a file 40x40 pixels. Make a circular selection by constraining the elliptical selection with the **Shift** key. Set the foreground to **dark green** and the background to **light green**. Using the **Gradient** tool set to **linear**, fill the selection a gradient starting at the lower-right corner and finishing at the upper-left corner. Then, **Select/Modify/Contract** by 3 pixels. Fill the selection with the same gradient going in the opposite direction.

Start with a file 40x40 pixels. Use the selection tool to create a square at least 1 pixel from the outside edge of the image. Set the foreground to **dark purple**, and the background to **light purple**. Fill the selection with a linear gradient, starting at the lower-right and finishing at the upper-left corner. Then **Select/Modify/Contract** by 3 pixels, and fill the selection with the same gradient going in the opposite direction.

Start with a file 40x40 pixels. Make an elliptical selection. Fill with magenta. Apply **Select/Modify/Contract** by 2 pixels, and **Select/Feather** at **1** pixel. Fill with dark magenta. Apply **Select/Modify/Contract** by 2 pixels again, and fill this selection with a gradation starting with magenta and ending with pink.

Start with a file 40x40 pixels. Select **dark gray** as the foreground color and **light gray** as the background color. Using the Gradient tool, fill the image with a gray linear gradation. Draw a 1-pixel black border all the way around the outside edge of the image. Make a light gray beveled edge at the top and left edges, as explained in the first example in this chapter. Draw a dark gray bevel at the bottom and right edges.

Start with an image 40x40 pixels. With the Lasso selection tool, create a triangular selection by **Alt+click** to constrain the selection to straight lines. Fill the triangular selection with dark blue. Apply **Select/Modify/Contract** by 4 pixels. Apply **Select/Feather** at 1 pixel, and fill the resulting smaller selection with light blue.

Start with an image 40x40 pixels. Use the Elliptical selection tool to create a circular selection, and fill with **red**. Apply **Select/Modify/Contract** by 3 pixels. Apply **Select/Feather** at 1 pixel, and fill with **yellow**. Repeat **Select/Modify/Contract** and **Select/Feather**, alternating red and yellow fills, until you reach the center.

Start with a file 40x40 pixels. With the foreground color set to **dark purple**, select the **Type** tool. Use a bold font (Futura Extra Black at 42 points was used in the example) and type a **question mark**. Apply **Select/None** (or **Ctrl+D**). Apply **Filter/Blur/Gaussian Blur** at **2.5** pixels. Set the foreground color to **white**, and again type the **question mark** in the same point size and style.

Using the textured icon created in this chapter, apply **Image/Adjust/Hue-Saturation**. Set the Hue to **+100**.

RECIPES FOR PHOTOPAINT

Start with a file 40x40 pixels. Fill with a **light gray** color. Then apply **Effects/Noise/Add Noise**, set to **Uniform**. Then apply **Effects/2D/Wind**, with the Opacity set to **40**, and the Strength set to **10**. Apply the **Wind** effect two more times. Finish the icon by drawing a 1-pixel black line at the edge, and a dark gray bevel as described in the textured icon example.

Start with a file 40x40 pixels. Draw a black 1-pixel line at the outer edge of the image. Then apply **Effects/3D/Emboss**, with the Emboss Color set to **gray**, the Depth set to **1**, and the Direction set to the **lower right**.

Start with a 40x40 pixel image. Double-click on the **Fill** tool to open the Fill roll-up. Select **Texture** fill, and select **Edit**. Change the Texture Library to **Samples**, and select **Purple Haze**. Fill the image. Next, apply **Effects/Artistic/Vignette**, with the Vignette Mode set to **black**, and the fade to **75**.

Start with a 40x40 pixel image. Double-click on the **Fill** tool to open the Fill roll-up. Select the **Texture Fill** icon, and then select **Edit**. Change the Texture Library to **Samples**, and select **Clouds**, **Morning**. Apply **Mask/All**, then **Mask/Feather**, with a Width, **6**; Direction, **inside**; and Edges, **soft**. Apply **Mask/Invert**, and **Effects/Color Adjust/Brightness-Intensity-Contrast**. Change the Brightness to **-30**.

Start with an image 100x40 pixels. Fill with **lavender**. Apply **Mask/All**, then **Mask/Shape/Reduce** by 3. Apply **Mask/Feather**, Width, **5**; Direction, **inside**; and Edges, **soft**. Next, apply **Mask, Invert**. Using the Fill roll-up, select **Fountain** fill. Select a square two-color fill from dark purple to **lavender**, and fill the mask.

Start with an image 50x50 pixels. Double-click on the **Fill** tool to open the Fill roll-up. Select the **Gradient Fill** icon, and apply **edit**. Create a linear gradient from light gray to dark gray. Next, select the **Rectangle** tool. Make sure the pen width is set to **zero**, and create a square, offset to the lower right within the image. Apply **Effects/Blur/Gaussian**, with a **2-pixel** radius. Change the Gradient fill to a **light yellow to ochre gradation**. Use the **Rectangle** tool to create a square that overlaps the Gray icon, as shown in the example.

Begin with a 40x40 pixel image. Double-click on the **Rectangle** tool, and set the Roundness to **15**, and check the **anti-aliasing** checkbox. Create a linear gradient from dark magenta to pink, at a 130° angle. Apply **Mask/Shape/Reduce** by **3** pixels, and apply the same **magenta to pink gradient** at a 45° angle.

Start with a 40x100 pixel image. Double-click on the **Rectangle** tool, and set the Roundness to **100**, and check the **anti-aliasing** checkbox. Select a linear gradient fill from light blue to **dark blue**. Apply **Effects/3D Effects/Emboss**. Select **Emboss Color**, **Original Color**; Depth, **1** pixel; Direction, to the **upper left**. Apply the same filter a second time by selecting **Effects** from the menu bar. Emboss, as the last filter used, will appear at the top of the Effects menu.

Begin with an image 100x40 pixels. Use the Freehand Mask tool to draw an irregular selection. Create a yellow to orange gradation at 130° and fill the mask. Apply **Mask/Shape/Reduce** by **5** pixels. Apply **Mask/Feather** to **1** pixel. Use the same gradation at 45° angle to fill the mask. Set the fill to **black** and use the Text tool to add anti-aliased text. Apply **Object/Combine/All Objects with Background** to save.

 Using the textured icon shown in this chapter, apply **Effects/Color Adjust/Hue-Saturation-Lightness**. Set the Hue to **-128**.

Chapter 4

CREATING SEAMLESS PATTERN TILES, OR WHY SEAMS ARE THE VISIBLE PANTY LINES OF GRAPHICS

I love making "seamless" pattern tiles, because it's so easy, (once you learn the tricks) to be able to make a gorgeous background in a matter of minutes. Working in a small format gives you a great excuse to experiment with colors and filters and textures.

A background pattern can be a great way to repeat a theme for your website. It can also be a good place to introduce subtle elements and color to your website.

What do I mean by seamless? If you're creating a background pattern tile that will be repeated, the edges are usually very noticeable. The seams where the pattern repeats are annoying and distracting, especially now that it has been pointed it out to you. Once you've mastered anti-aliasing and seamless pattern tile creation, you become an honorary member of the Web Graphics Police. Seeing jagged edges on type and obvious seams on repeated patterns will probably make you edgy.

Luckily, there are a number of ways to eliminate and avoid those pesky seams. Following the tutorial, you'll find a number of recipes for seamless pattern tiles. I should warn you, though, that creating pattern tiles can be addictive.

You'll want to remember that not all browsers, at this point, will display a tiled background. Browsers that don't display background patterns will display the browser's default color, usually gray or white.

One of the main things to remember when you've created your seamless background is that text must be legible over the top of your pattern. You don't need to worry about that now, since I'll discuss decreasing the contrast in images in Chapter Five.

PHOTOSHOP: CREATING A SEAMLESS PATTERN TILE

The following steps will show you how to create a seamless pattern tile in Photoshop:

1 Start with a new file, 96x96 pixels, RGB Color (Figure 4.1). Select **light blue** as a foreground color and **dark blue** as a background color. Apply **Filter/Render/Clouds**. Instant sky!

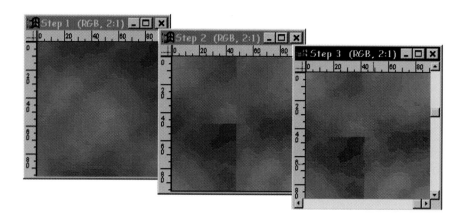

Figure 4.1 Creating a seamless pattern tile in Photoshop

2 There are probably seams in the image you've just created. To check, use **Filter/Other/Offset**, with the **Wrap Around** radio button checked. The amounts are 48 and 48 (see Figure 4.2). This way, the seam will appear through the middle of the image, where it will be easier to see and to clean up.

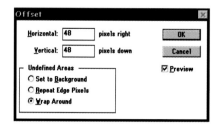

Figure 4.2 Offset filter dialog box

3 There are now a number of ways to clean up that ugly seam. Many people use the cloning brush, but I prefer to use the Smudge tool. It's a lot like finger painting. Just drag the Smudge tool, set to a small or medium brush size, across the center seam a couple of times.

4 Another way to clean up those seams is to grab a piece of the image and copy it and paste it over the seam. Use the Lasso selection tool to make a small, irregular selection. Apply **Select/Feather** at **2** pixels. Apply **Edit/Copy**, (or **Ctrl+C**), **Edit/Paste** (or **Ctrl+V**), and drag or nudge (using the arrow keys) the patch over a seam. Continue patching until all the seams are covered.

A third method to clean up pattern tile edges is to use a paint tool. Since this pattern tile is made up of a very soft texture, you can clean up the seams using the Airbrush tool set to a medium brush size.

5 Now, fill a larger selection to check how your image will look as a background. Open a new file (or **Ctrl+N**), set to 300x300 pixels. Return to the seamless tile you've created. Apply **Select/All** (or **Ctrl+A**), **Edit/Define Pattern** as shown in Figure 4.3.

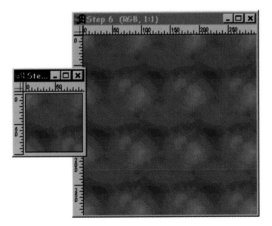

Figure 4.3 Applying a pattern as a fill

6 Select the new file, and apply **Edit/ Fill**. Within the Fill dialog box, select Use, **Pattern**; Opacity, **100%**; and Mode, **Normal**. If you see any obvious seams when the tile is repeated, you can clean them up in the original file, using the smudge tool or the patch method.

PHOTOPAINT: CREATING A SEAMLESS PATTERN TILE

The following steps show you how to create a seamless pattern in PhotoPaint:

1 Start with a new file, 96x96 pixels, 24-bit color. Double-click on the **Fill** tool to open the Fill roll-up. Select the **Texture Fill** icon, and use the default fill (Rain Drops Soft 3C, from the Styles Library), as shown in Figure 4.4.

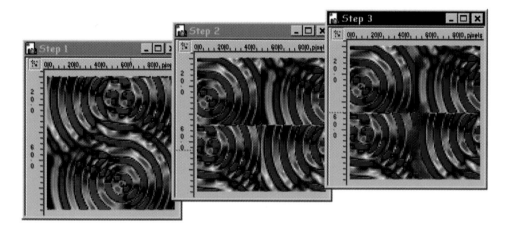

Figure 4.4 Creating a seamless pattern tile in PhotoPaint

2 Now, apply the **Offset** filter so that you can clean up any unsightly edges. Apply **Effects/2D/Offset**, with the Horizontal and Vertical values set to **50**, and the **Wrap Around** radio button selected.

3 Start to clean up the edges by double-clicking the **Effect** tool, to open the Tool Settings roll-up. Select Smudge, **4** pixel size; Transparency, **5**; Soft Edge, **0**. You may want to save this smudge brush for later use on other web projects. Select the **Save Brush** button and name the brush you've created.

Next, smudge the vertical edge by using the Smudge brush. If the pattern you're trying to make seamless has an obvious pattern, it helps to follow the pattern with the smudge. In this case, you can curve the stroke of the smudge brush to mimic the rings.

4 There are a number of ways to clean up edges. Use the Freehand Mask tool, and select an irregular area. Apply **Mask/Feather**; Width, **3**; Direction, **Inside**; Edges, **Soft**; **Copy** (or **Ctrl+C**) and **Paste As Object** (or **Ctrl+V**). Drag the copy into position to cover the horizontal edge, as shown in Figure 4.5. In addition, you could use the paint tool to cover up the edges.

Figure 4.5 Covering a seam with a feathered mask

5 Next, save the tile you've created.

6 To see how the pattern tile you have just created will look when it's repeated, open a new file, 300x300 pixels. Double-click on the **Fill** tool to open the Fill roll-up. Select the **Bitmap Fill** icon. Select **Edit**, and select the tile you've just saved (Figure 4.6).

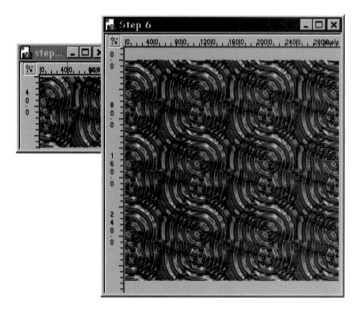

Figure 4.6 Using a pattern as a fill

PhotoPaint's Coolest Tool, Terrazzo

PhotoPaint really excels in creating seamless pattern tiles, thanks to the Terrazzo filter that is built into PhotoPaint. If you're familiar with quilt patterns, you'll understand the way in which Terrazzo creates a seamless pattern tile. It takes a geometric shape and repeats it, similar to the way that quilt patterns repeat. From one file, you can make dozens of unique seamless pattern tiles. But enough talking, let's play!

You'll want to start with an image, which can be a photo, a drawing, anything you want (Figure 4.7). Once you've opened your image, apply **Effects/Artistic/ Terrazzo**.

Figure 4.7 Terrazzo dialog box

By dragging the selection tool within the Terrazzo dialog box, you select the area you would like to see tiled. Click on the **Symmetry** icon, and you'll have a number of choices for the how you would like the selection repeated. The patterns for the geometrical repetition are named after quilt patterns, such as Honey Bees and Card Tricks.

You can play with the Feather slider, too, to soften the transitions. When you find a pattern that you like, just use the Save Tile button.

As an example of the versatility of Terrazzo, Figure 4.8 shows twenty patterns created from the previous image.

Figure 4.8 Seamless patterns created using Terrazzo

There are 75 filters included with PhotoPaint version 6.0, which means you can create an endless number of unique patterns by simply applying a filter or two to an image, and then using Terrazzo.

In addition, if you double-click on the **Fill** tool to bring up the Fill roll-up, and select **Bitmap Fills/Edit/Load**, you can import the hundreds of seamless photographic pattern tiles that Corel packed into version 6. They're on CD number one, in the folder named Tiles. Once you've selected a tile, be sure to check the **Scale Pattern to Fit** checkbox. Then fill your image, and the pattern will tile seamlessly.

VARIOUS TILING TIPS

Although all of the example tiles in this chapter are square, there is no reason why you can't create a rectangular tile. As a matter of fact, sometimes it makes more sense, particularly in the interest of creating a smaller file, to create a very long and narrow tile. If, for instance, you wanted a background of simple various colored vertical stripes, you could create a file that was 1 pixel high by 500 pixels across, and your stripes would tile seamlessly.

I haven't discussed *transparency* or *interlacing* yet (see Chapter Eight), but you emphatically don't want to use either of these gif options on a background tile. Interlacing the background tile will delay everything on the page from loading until the background image has finished loading. There is no reason to use transparency with a background image.

There are a number of fun things to experiment with when you create seamless pattern tiles. Sometimes the Noise filter, followed by the Emboss filter, can result in some nice paper effects. A little noise can also obscure obvious pixelation or other minor defects in your image.

Seamless pattern tiles are useful for a lot more than just background patterns. If you save your tile in bmp format, you'll be able to load it as a background for Windows. To load your bmp file, right-click anywhere on the desktop, and select **Properties**. This will open the Display Properties window. You can select **Browse** to find your pattern. Be sure to select the **Tile** radio button, and you should see a preview of what your pattern tile will look like as wallpaper.

In addition to Windows wallpaper, you can use seamless pattern tiles as bump and texture maps for 3D objects as well, if you're into 3D modeling.

RECIPES FOR SEAMLESS PATTERNS IN PHOTOSHOP

Note: All of the following recipes for patterns start with an RGB file 96x96 pixels.

Fill with light blue. Apply **Filter/Noise/Add Noise**, Amount, **60**; Distribution, **Uniform**. Apply **Filter/Pixelate/Facet**.

Fill with violet. Change foreground color to magenta. Use a small-size paintbrush to scribble. Apply **Filter/Other/Offset**. Apply **Filter/Stylize/Diffuse**.

Fill with pale yellow. Change the foreground color to ochre. Scribble with a small paintbrush. Apply **Filter/Other/Offset**. Next, apply **Filter/Noise/Dust and Scratches**; Radius, **4** pixels; Threshold, **0**. Apply **Filter/Noise/Add Noise**; Amount, **30**.

Fill with light gray. Apply **Filter/Noise/Add Noise**. Change the foreground color to a medium gray, and use the Type tool to add "Cool" at 36 point size. Apply **Select/All** (or **Ctrl+A**). Apply **Filter/Other/Offset**, and add "stuff!" at 36 points.

Fill with light gray. Apply **Filter/Noise/Add Noise**. Apply **Filter/Blur/Radial Blur**; Blur Amount, **10**; Blur Method, **Spin**; Quality, **Good**.

Fill with light blue. Apply **Filter/Noise/Add Noise**. Apply **Noise/Median**; Radius, **2**. Apply **Filter/Other/Offset**. Apply **Noise/Median**; Radius, **2**.

Draw vertical stripes using a small paintbrush. You can constrain the paintbrush to a straight line by using the Shift key. The stripes don't need to be perfect. Apply **Filter/Distort/Ripple**; Size, **Small**; Amount, **230**.

Using the rippled stripe tile (above), apply **Filter/Stylize/Emboss**; angle, **135**; Height, **3** pixels; Amount, **100%**. Apply **Filter/Stylize/Diffuse**; Mode, **Normal**.

Beginning with a striped tile, apply **Filter/Noise/Add Noise**; Amount, **130**. Next, apply **Filter/Noise/Dust and Scratches**; Radius, **4**; Threshold, **0**.

Fill the image with yellow. Paint magenta stripes using the paintbrush tool. Apply **Filter/Blur/Radial Blur**; Amount, **72**; Blur Method, **Spin**; Quality, **Good**. Apply **Filter/Other/Offset**; Horizontal Offset, **48** pixels; Vertical Offset, **48** pixels; **Wrap Around**. Clean up the edges with the Smudge tool as described earlier in this chapter.

Photoshop

RECIPES FOR SEAMLESS PATTERNS IN PHOTOPAINT

Note: All of the following recipes for patterns start with a 24-bit RGB file 96x96 pixels.

Double-click on the **Fill** tool to open the fill Tool Settings roll-up. Select **Bitmap Fill/Edit**. Click on the colored tile to scroll through more tile examples. Select the tile shown above. Check the **Scale Pattern to Fit** checkbox. Apply **Effects/2D/Edge Detect**; Background Color, **Black**; Sensitivity, **2**.

Double-click on the **Fill** tool to open the fill Tool Settings roll-up. Select **Bitmap Fill/Edit/Import**. Using the CD labeled Disk 1 from Corel 6, select **Tiles/Nature/Nature06m.cpt**. Check the **Scale Pattern to Fit** checkbox. Apply **Effects/Noise/Add Noise** using Color Noise.

Fill with brown using Uniform Fill or select the color from the palette at the bottom of the screen using the right mouse button. Apply **Effects/Artistic/Canvas**. Load the file stuccoc.pcx from the Canvas dialog box. Apply using the defaults.

Fill with purple using Uniform Fill or select the color from the palette at the bottom of the screen using the right mouse button. Apply **Effects/3D/Whirlpool**, using the Rings Style preset. Apply **Effects/2D/Offset**, and use the Smudge tool to clean up the edges as explained earlier in this chapter.

Fill with yellow using Uniform Fill or select the color from the palette at the bottom of the screen using the right mouse button. Apply **Effects/Noise/Add Noise**, select **Color Noise**; Level, **50**; Density, **50**; **Uniform**. Apply **Effects/2D/Pixelate**, Pixelate Mode, **Rectangular**; Width, **10**; Height, **10**; Opacity **70%**.

Fill with pale blue using Uniform Fill or select the color from the palette at the bottom of the screen using the right mouse button. Apply **Effects/Artistic/Alchemy**. Apply the **Pointillist Style**.

Fill with green using Uniform Fill or select the color from the palette at the bottom of the screen using the right mouse button. Apply **Effects/Artistic/Vignette**; Vignette Mode, **Black**; Offset, **0**; Fade, **75**. Next, apply **Effects/Artistic/Alchemy**; Style, **Planet Paint**.

Double-click on the **Fill** tool to open the fill Tool Settings roll-up. Select **Bitmap Fill/Edit/Import**. Using the CD labeled Disk 1 from Corel 6, select **Tiles/Food/Food15m.cpt**. Check the **Scale Pattern to Fit** checkbox. Next, apply **Effects/Color Transform/Solarize**; Level, **120**.

Apply **Effects/Render/Julia Explorer/Presets/Rainbow Twist**. The resulting pattern is not seamlessly tiled, so **Apply Effects/2D/Offset** at **50%**. Next apply **Effects/3D/Zigzag**; period, **50**; Strength, **50**; Damping, **50**. The resulting tile is seamless.

Fill with orange using Uniform Fill or select the color from the palette at the bottom of the screen using the right mouse button. Apply **Effects/Artistic/Alchemy**; Style, **Oil Canvas Blur**. Next, apply **Effects/3D/Emboss**, using Original Color; Depth, **2**; Direction, **lower right**.

PhotoPaint

PART 2:
INTERMEDIATE WEB
GRAPHICS

USING COLOR AND BRINGING DOWN CONTRAST, OR NOT INDUCING PAINFUL MIGRAINES IN YOUR READERS

A recent visitor to my website told me that he was grateful to find my Photoshop tips. He had ended up on Mirsky's Worst of The Web (http://mirsky.turnpike.net/wow/Worst.html) because of the graphics at his website. Public humiliation can be a great motivation for improvement.

You've spent the last few chapters learning how to create specific types of images. It's time to take a step back and start thinking about page design. I won't be discussing HTML here, because there are many other books that cover HTML very well. Instead, the layout of the web age is the focus, as well as how the different elements fit together. This chapter also addresses troubleshooting design problems on a web page. To begin with, however, I discuss using color for emphasis, mood, and unity.

USING COLOR FOR EMPHASIS

Color can be a wonderful tool or a deadly weapon. In my first two years of art school, we worked only in black and white. The theory was that we weren't educated enough to deal with color, and it was best to learn the basics of drawing and painting in black and white without the distraction of color. Although this was frustrating, it was still a good way to learn. Working in black and white forces you to focus on the artwork design.

Obviously, nobody is learning web graphics this way. (Well, you also don't attend life drawing classes, so I guess it all evens out.) You have the full range of color available from the first time that you open up Photoshop or PhotoPaint. But just because you have 16 million colors doesn't mean that you should use them all in the same image. Color can be used to organize and emphasize; unfortunately, it can also confuse and distract.

If you have a web page that just isn't working, there are a few things you can do to check your page design.

Look at the page in grayscale, rather than in color. By seeing your design in grayscale, you won't be distracted by color. Any problems with light and dark contrast and legibility will be instantly apparent.

Figures 5.1 and 5.2 show that the only legible part of the page is the heading "Adrian's Amazing Bean Dip." The background pattern is so busy and so dark that you can't read the text at all.

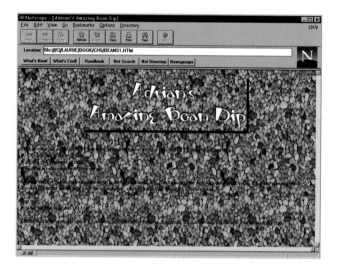

Figure 5.1 An unreadable web page.

Figure 5.2 Looking at the web page in grayscale.

You can convert your web page to grayscale by taking a screenshot of your web page. This is a simple thing to accomplish, but few people seem to know how to take a screen shot, making it one of the great secrets of the PC. With your web page visible, press the **Print Scrn** key on your keyboard. This copies a picture of your screen to the Windows clipboard. Open a paint program. In Photoshop, select **File/New**, **Edit/Paste**. In PhotoPaint, use **Edit/Paste As New Document**. Now, you'll want to convert your screenshot to grayscale. In Photoshop, apply **Mode/Grayscale**. In PhotoPaint, use **Image/Convert To/Grayscale**.

Check to see what first draws your eye. Your eye will go to the page area that has the most contrast. Is this the most important element? Can the page use more contrast? Less contrast? Are the elements (text, buttons, etc.) organized logically? Is it easy to find important information?

In the Amazing Bean Dip example in Figure 5.3, the only change that was made was to lighten the background, thus making the text legible. The title is the first item to draw your attention, and the recipe is now easy to read.

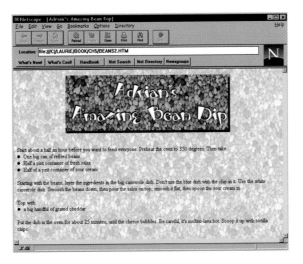

Figure 5.3 Changing the contrast of the background.

I try to avoid using horizontal lines that divide a web page because the lines usually will draw your eye before anything else on the page. Since the horizontal line is usually the least important page element, I try to find other ways to organize information. Often, the information is better presented if it is placed on separate, linked pages, rather than being placed on the same page and divided by a horizontal line.

If your page works well in grayscale, usually it will work well in color, too. If you're confused about using color, and even if you aren't, a *limited palette* is helpful. On a limited palette, all of the colors are related. For example, maybe you'll want to limit your colors to mostly blues, as shown in Figure 5.4. That means greenish blues, aquamarines, navy blues, and blue violets, and violets. It also means using pale blues and deep dark blues.

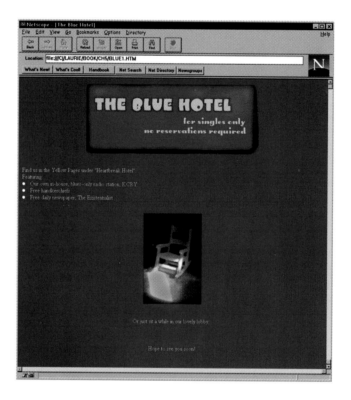

Figure 5.4 Using a limited palette.

Working in a limited color palette can help your page design in the following ways:

- Using a dominant color establishes a mood and can tie dissimilar elements together visually.

- Using a limited palette means that if you'll be saving your graphics in the .gif file format, you'll be able to index to a smaller number of colors, thus creating a smaller file, which will load more quickly. Note that when you save in the gif file format, you can specify how many colors you want to reduce the graphic to. This is called *indexing*.

Using a dominant color can establish to the viewer that all your pages are linked. You could also use a different dominant color on separate pages to establish clearly their different identities. For example, if you're designing a cooking website, the page about appetizers could be red, your main dish page could be violet, and so on. That way, visitors would have a clearer sense of where they are within your site.

After designing your page with a dominant color, using a contrasting color will *really* draw attention. You can see that the yellow "new" graphic jumps right out on the blue hotel page in Figure 5.5.

Figure 5.5 A touch of yellow for contrast.

USING COLOR TO SET A TONE

When you begin to design a web page, you'll want to think about the over all color. Sometimes this is the most difficult part of designing for me. I'll often look through books and magazines to find a color combination that suits the mood and feeling of the artwork that I'm designing. I might find the right color combination in a landscape, a fabric, or a painting.

Color can also have emotional connotations and expectations. When red, white, and blue are used together, it has a connection to American patriotism. Black and red used together can convey violence as illustrated in Figure 5.6, whereas pastels can symbolize pleasant tranquillity.

Figure 5.6 Selecting color appropriate for the subject matter.

If you get feedback from people that a graphic or page isn't working or is some-how disturbing, you might want to consider whether or not the colors you're using are inappropriate such as the pastel Dracula Web site in Figure 5.7.

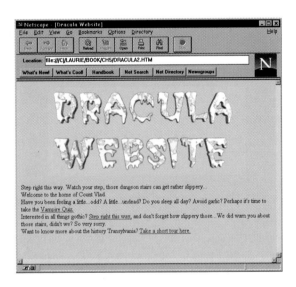

Figure 5.7 A different color choice.

There's no reason that you can't use any of this information on color to break the rules. Creating a page on chaos and dissonance? Maybe you want to use as many of the 16 million colors as possible.

When you are trying to make a decision about a color scheme for you web-site, try to decide on a single dominant color first, and choose the secondary colors later. Once you've set the tone with the dominant color, other choices should be easier.

Often, there are colors that you have to use on a website, yet want to de-emphasize. For instance, if you are designing a company website and the compa-ny logo is an eye-jarring chartreuse, you'll want to play the color down. You can often lessen a color's impact by surrounding it with a softer, paler version of itself. In the case of the chartreuse logo, placing it against a pale green background will decrease the impact of the chartreuse.

Hexing Colors

Okay, so you've decided on the colors you want to use for your page background and text. You will need to know the hex codes for the colors to specify in the html for your page. The HTML code for specifying a black background color with white text will look like this:

```
<BODY BGCOLOR="#000000" Text="#FFFFFF">
```

Not all browsers will display a background color or text color that you specify in this way. To help you find the hex codes for the colors that you've chosen, you can use a shareware utility, or visit a website that will figure out the hex codes for you, or you can use the Windows calculator. Another great secret of the PC revealed!

First, find out the RGB number for the colors you want to find the hex codes for. In Photoshop, use the Eyedropper tool to select the color you want to use for text or background. Double-click on the foreground color in the Tool palette, which will open the **Color Picker**. You will find the RGB value for the color.

To find the RGB value in PhotoPaint, use the Eyedropper tool to select the color. Double-click on the **Current Fill** swatch at the bottom of the screen. You'll find the RGB value in the dialog box that opens.

Now, open the Windows Calculator, as shown in Figure 5.8. Don't bother to close the paint program you're in; this is multitasking! From the **Start** button, select **Programs/Accessories/Calculator**. On the Calculator's menu, select View/Scientific.

Figure 5.8 The Windows calculator.

You have three numbers, one each for Red, Green, and Blue. In this example, R=39, G=5, and B=85. Select the **DEC** radio button (stands for decimal), and using the keypad, enter **39**, the number for Red. Now, select the **HEX** radio button. Voila—the first two digits of your color's hex code, **27**. Select **CE** (**Clear Entry**), and **DEC**, and enter the Green value, **5**. You will find that the hex value is also **5**. Since this is a single digit, we'll want to add a zero, so that you end up with six digits for the entire hex code. Use **CE** and **DEC**, and enter the Blue value, **85**. The hex code is **55**. So, the final six-digit hex code will be 270555.

If you would prefer to visit a website to select your hex codes, you can visit any of the following websites:

Thalia's Guide: Compose Page Color: http://www.sci.kun.nl/

ColorMaker: http://www.missouri.edu/~c588349/colormaker.html

HYPE Electrazine - The Color Specifier:
http://www.users.interport.net/~giant/COLOR/hype_color.html

Beach Rat: http://www.novalink.com/pei/hex/hex.html

The following two WYSIWYG HTML editors also feature a color selector that inserts the hex code into your HTML:

NaviPress: http://www.navisoft.com

WEBWizard: http://www.halcyon.com/artamedia/webwizard

Hex Color Chart

Color	Color Name	RGB	Hex Code
	White	255/255/255	#ffffff
	Black	0/0/0	#000000
	Deep Gray	63/63/63	#3f3f3f
	Pale Gray	191/191/191	#bfbfbf
	Flame Red	255/0/0/	#ff0000
	Pale Red	255/230/230	#ffe6e6
	Russett	113/0/0	#710000
	Peach	255/189/189	#ffbdbd
	Deep Magenta	120/10/50	#780a32
	Rose	200/20/90	#c8145a
	Cobalt	60/0/120	#3c0078
	Pale Blue Violet	200/200/255	#c8c8ff
	True Blue	0/0/255	#0000ff
	Pale Blue	210/210/255	#d2d2ff
	Teal	0/80/90	#00505a
	Aqua	0/200/200	#00c8c8
	Pale Aqua	200/250/250	#c8fafa
	Hunters Green	0/70/0	#004600
	Grass Green	0/180/0	#00b400
	Pale Green	210/255/210	#d2ffd2
	Pale Yellow	255/255/210	#ffffd2
	Gold	180/140/0	#b48c00
	Pale Gold	255/235/150	#ffeb96
	Deep Sienna	80/20/0	#501400
	Pumpkin	220/100/0	#dc6400
	Pale Orange	255/220/180	#ffdcb4

NOTE: Due to the limitations of printing RGB colors, the color chart may not accurately reflect the RGB colors on your monitor.

PHOTOSHOP: CHANGING CONTRAST

In the last chapter, you created some wonderful seamless pattern tiles. Unfortunately (see Figure 5.9), some of them are completely unusable as background tiles because they overwhelm the type that will go on top of them.

Figure 5.9 The tile before lightening

1 Open the second example from the recipes in Chapter Four. Select **Image/Adjust/Levels**. Drag the **Output Levels** black slider from the left side toward the center. You will see that the tile lightens as you do this. If you wanted to create a very dark tile, so that you could add white text over the top, you would want to drag the white slider toward the center.

2 You're going to temporarily add some text to this tile, to see if it has been lightened enough. Select **Window/Show Layers**. From the flyout menu on the Layers palette, select **New Layer**. You can name the layer **Type** (see Figure 5.10).

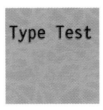

Figure 5.10 Testing the adjusted tile

3 Use the Type tool to add text to the Type Layer. We've used Layers for this example so that we can manipulate the type and background separately. If the tile still seems too dark, you can select the **Background Layer**, and return to **Image/Adjust/Levels**. When the contrast seems right, discard the Type Layer by dragging the Type Layer to the **trashcan** icon. Save your tile (Figure 5.11).

Figure 5.11 The lightened tile

PHOTOPAINT: CHANGING CONTRAST

In Chapter Four, we created some great seamless pattern tiles to use as backgrounds on web pages. Until we lower the contrast on the pattern tiles, type won't be legible when placed on top of the patterns. Using PhotoPaint, we will correct the legibility problem.

1 Open the third example from the PhotoPaint recipes in Chapter Four. Apply **Effects/Color Adjust/Brightness-Contrast-Intensity**; Brightness, **50**; Contrast, **50**; Intensity, **0**. You want to raise the brightness and lower the contrast in this tile.

To make this a very dark tile, you could lower the Brightness and Contrast values, as shown in Figure 5.12.

Figure 5.12 The tile before lightening

2 Add some type to the tile using the Type tool. If you think the tile isn't light enough, you can apply the **Brightness-Contrast-Intensity** filter again, as shown in Figure 5.13. When the tile looks right, delete the type and save your tile.

Figure 5.13 Testing the adjusted tile

CHAPTER

SCANNING FOR THE WEB, OR BRINGING CONTRAST UP, AND LOOKING GOOD AT LOW RESOLUTION

Sooner or later, you will have to deal with a bad scan. Luckily, making a bad scan look better is not that difficult with Photoshop or PhotoPaint. Some good tools are available to help you adjust, cover up, delete, or compensate for almost every bad scanning situation.

When scanning keep in mind the following advice. First, it's usually better to scan the photo or artwork for the Web at a higher than screen resolution, and then resample down to the size you'll want to work at. Try scanning at 200 to 300 dpi. This means that you'll start with an image that has 200 or 300 pixels per inch, and end up with an image at screen resolution, or 96 pixels per inch.

I try to keep artwork to a width of 500 pixels or less. The three most common screen resolutions for PC's are 640x480, 800x600, and 1040x768. Using a width of 640 pixels, and taking into account the menu bars for the web browser that the website is viewed on, 500 pixels means that most people won't have to scroll horizontally to see the entire graphic.

The most common problem with scans is that they have lost their original contrast. The darks seem a little faded, and the whites are often dingy and gray looking. You'll learn how to bring back the contrast in a very poor scan, and add an interesting background as the first project in this chapter.

Figure 6.1

Figure 6.2

Figure 6.3

Figure 6.4

Figure 6.1 The original photograph.
Figure 6.2 Dust and Scratches filter used on background.
Figure 6.3 Unsharp Mask filter used.
Figure 6.4 Add Noise filter applied to background.

Each scan will have its own individual problems that you'll need to compensate for. Figure 6.1 shows the original, unfiltered scan.

The **Dust and Scratches** filter works by averaging out surrounding pixels to cover a small error; it can also be used to blur an area. A selection was created for the background area in the second example (Figure 6.2), and the Dust and Scratches filter was used.

Another indispensable filter for scans is **Unsharp Mask**. The Unsharp Mask actually sharpens details and edges, contrary to its name. In the third example (Figure 6.3), the Unsharp Mask Filter was applied only to the little boy, and not to the background.

Sometimes using the **Noise** filter can help clear up graininess, and other irregularities on the scan. It's a good last-ditch effort filter. In the fourth example (Figure 6.4), the Noise filter was applied only to the background. The tools within Photoshop or PhotoPaint also come in handy when dealing with scans.

If you have a scan with a number of errors in the sky for example, you might want to use a cloning brush to cover the problem areas with a copy of the sky from a different portion of your photo. Cloning can look more natural than trying to paint over a problem using the paintbrush or airbrush.

The second project in this chapter, colorizing a grayscale version of a scan, can enliven an otherwise mediocre photograph. It's also one of the most frequently asked questions that I get at my website. However, you must promise to never use the colorizing techniques on lovely old black and white movies.

You will be saving all of the scans in jpeg format. The jpeg file format is a 24-bit, lossy compression format. That means that a jpeg can handle a greater range of colors more smoothly than the gif file format, which is an 8-bit compression file format. Jpeg is lossy, which means that some information is lost during the compression process, and it's always a good idea to keep a 24-bit uncompressed copy of your image for this reason.

For photographs, a jpeg file is almost always a much smaller file than a gif file would be. For example, the jukebox at my website is a 50K file saved in jpeg format. As a gif file, the jukebox is 200K, and much more dithered and less appealing. If you're concerned about browsers that don't support jpegs, you can always offer a link to a page with a gif file on it. At this point, there are very few browsers that don't support jpegs. It's worth your time to experiment with the different jpeg settings to see what you consider acceptable quality.

PHOTOSHOP: FIXING A BAD SCAN

1 Using the Rectangular selection tool, select the area of the scan you wish to keep (see Figure 6.5). Select **Edit/Crop**.

Figure 6.5 The original scan in Photoshop

2 Next, compensate for dingy whites and dull darks. Apply **Image/Adjust/Levels**. To darken the dark areas, drag the left Input Slider toward the center. To lighten the light areas, drag the right Input Slider toward the center. Every scan will be different, so you'll need to watch the preview as you adjust the sliders. In this particular scan, the dark areas looked fine, but the light areas needed to be lightened (see Figure 6.6).

Figure 6.6 Adjust/Levels used to lighten the scan

3 Select the background area and fill it with a pattern fill to make this scan more interesting. The background is very complex because of all of the hair in the photo. Using the selection tool, and holding down the **Shift** key, make two or three selections from different parts of the photo. Next, apply **Select/Similar**. Everything in the photo that is similar to the selected areas will be made part of the selection. If not enough of the background has been selected, **Undo** (**Ctrl+Z**) and double-click on the **Magic Wand** to open the Magic Wand Options palette. Increase the Tolerance number and apply **Select/Similar** again.

In Figure 6.7, the bits of cropped toys I wanted to delete were added to the selection by holding down the **Shift** key and using the selection tool. As the final step in making this complex selection, apply **Select/Feather** at **3** pixels.

Figure 6.7 Using Select/Similar to create a complex selection

4 Open one of the seamless pattern tile files you created in Chapter Four. Apply **Select/All**, then **Edit/Define Pattern**. Returning to the scanned image, select **Edit/Fill/Pattern**. Save the file as a jpeg, using the Medium Quality setting. Figure 6.8, which is 450x273 pixels, was less than 30K when saved using the jpeg format.

Figure 6.8 A pattern fill applied to the background

PHOTOSHOP: COLORIZING A GRAYSCALE PHOTO

I'm going to start with a color photo, and add some mood and warmth by hand-coloring it (see Figure 6.9). This is not a bad photo—it has good contrast, and it's in focus.

Figure 6.9 The original scan in Photoshop

1 Select the area of the photo you want to keep, using the Rectangular selection tool, and apply **Edit/Crop**. Next, apply **Mode/Grayscale**. A dialog box will ask if you want to discard the color information. Select **OK**.

2 Apply **Image/Adjust/Levels**. Since you will be adding color over this grayscale photo, you will want to lighten it a little so that the photo doesn't become too dark. Drag the right Input Level slider toward the center, and apply. Next, apply **Mode/RGB Color** (Figure 6.10).

Figure 6.10 Image's Mode changed to grayscale

3 Open the Layers palette, and from the Flyout menu, select **New Layer**. Change the Mode to **Multiply**. This way, the grayscale photo will be visible through the color you apply.

4 Select the **Airbrush** tool, and set it to a large size. From the Options palette, set the Pressure to **20%** or less. In this photo, I painted in the background first.

Don't worry about being sloppy or painting outside the lines. You can always delete the layer you're applying color to and start over with a new layer. You also don't need to individually color each item in the photo (Figure 6.11).

Figure 6.11 Finished colorized photo

5 From the Layers Flyout menu, select **Flatten** to combine the layers. Save the file as a Medium Quality jpeg.

PHOTOPAINT: FIXING A BAD SCAN

1 Here's another scan with a case of the uglies (Figure 6.12). Using the Cropping tool, select the area of the scan you wish to keep. Double-click inside the area you want to crop to, or use the right mouse button, and select **Crop To Selection**. Select **Image/Resample; Process, anti-alias** to change the size of the scan.

Figure 6.12 The original scan in PhotoPaint

2 Next, compensate for those pesky dingy, dull whites and flat darks. Apply **Effects/Color Adjust/Brightness-Contrast-Intensity**. For this scan, you want to raise the brightness and contrast quite a bit. Every scan will be different. Use the preview and experiment.

3 Well, the scan is still nothing to write home about. Sometimes adding an interesting background helps. Select some of the background using a masking tool. Apply **Mask/Similar**. To adjust the range of color selected, double-click on the **Magic Wand** masking tool and raise or lower the Tolerance. Apply **Mask/Feather**; Direction, **Outside**; Feather, **3**; Edges, **Soft**.

To add to the mask, select the **+** icon from the toolbar, or **Mask/Mode/Add** to Mask.

4 Apply **Effects/Artistic/Alchemy**; Style, **Bubbles Grid**. The selection will be filled with a pattern of bubbles, as shown in Figure 6.13. Save the file as a jpeg file. You can choose a compression ratio between 2 and 255. I've found that a level of 60 to 100 is a good range for web images.

Figure 6.13 A pattern fill used in the background

Once you've saved your file, you can check the file size by selecting **Image/Info**.

PHOTOPAINT: COLORIZING A GRAYSCALE PHOTO

I'm starting with a color photo for this project (see Figure 6.14). I could just as easily start with a line drawing (an old engraving, for example) or a black and white photo.

Figure 6.14 The original scan in PhotoPaint

1 As in the first PhotoPaint example, crop and resample if necessary. Apply **Effects/Color Adjust/Brightness-Contrast-Intensity**. Change the Brightness value to **20**. You're lightening the photo so that when the color is applied the photo won't become too dark.

2 Apply **Image/Convert To/Grayscale**. This removes the color information as shown in Figure 6.15. Apply **Image/Convert To/RGB Color** so that you can begin colorizing.

Figure 6.15 Image changed to grayscale

3 Double-click on the **Paintbrush** tool to open the Tool Settings palette. Select the **Airbrush, Type, Wide Cover; Paint, Multiply;** Transparency, **30**. Paint loosely.

4 Continue to paint, changing colors as necessary. When you're finished, save the file as a jpeg. In Figure 6.16, the waterfall was kept white so that it would remain the focus point for the photograph.

Figure 6.16 Finished colorized photo

chapter seven

Giving Graphics Interesting Edges, or There's More to Life Than Rectangles

A square is a rectangle, but a rectangle is not a square. You remember this from geometry class in the fourth grade, don't you? Well, sometimes even a rectangle shouldn't be a rectangle.

There's a tendency when designing web graphics to design right up to the corners of the image area. This means that every graphic may become a boring rectangle. If you're guilty of this, you're missing an opportunity to give your pages a more interesting look by changing the outside shape of your images.

In Chapter Five, I discussed how color can unify your web pages and give them a unique personality. Giving your graphics more interesting edges can also provide your pages a more dynamic yet unified look.

If you use some of these techniques, you may need to make more careful decisions about cropping your graphic. When you feather or texturize the edges important information can be lost. Note that you can use the methods and recipes in this chapter not just for header graphics and photos, but also for icons.

Speaking of geometry class, there's another hangover from grade school that comes into play when learning how to create web graphics. Because creating artwork is supposed to be fun and easy, I've found that people tend to blame themselves when they reach a plateau in the learning curve, or run into a problem with software. Art was always the easiest class in school, so why is this computer stuff sometimes difficult? Because learning about computer graphics often resembles math class more than art class. Remember to take breaks, and learn the **Ctrl+Z** keystroke. But I digress. On to the importance of not being rectangular all the time.

PHOTOSHOP: CREATIVE EDGES

The color that you select for the area surrounding an image should be the same color as the web page for the image. If your web page is light gray, then the area surrounding your image should be light gray instead of white as I've used in these examples.

1 Start with an image 200 pixels wide x 150 pixels tall (Figure 7.1). You can use a portion of a scan or a texture fill.

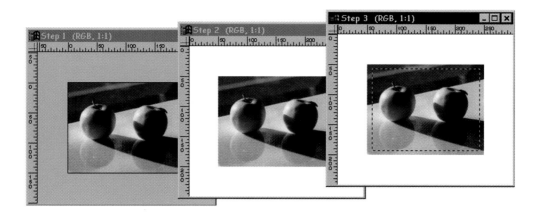

Figure 7.1 Creating an interesting edge in Photoshop

2 Set the background color to white. Apply **Image/Canvas Size**, using a width of 300 pixels, a height of 250 pixels. You may want to use Image/Duplicate at this point, if you want to try some of the other recipe variations on the same file.

3 Make a rectangular selection using the selection tool a little ways in from the edges of the image.

4 Apply **Select/Inverse** as shown in Figure 7.2.

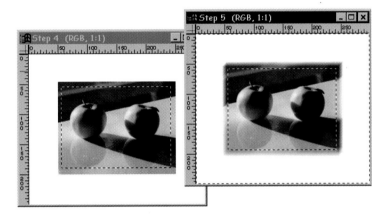

Figure 7.2 Applying a filter to create an interesting edge

5 Apply **Filter/Blur/Motion Blur**; Angle, **45**; Distance, **10**.

PHOTOPAINT: CREATIVE EDGES

The color that you select for the area surrounding an image should be the same color as the web page for the image. If your web page is light gray, then the area surrounding your image should be light gray instead of white as I've used in these examples.

1 Start with an image 200 pixels wide x 150 pixels tall. You can use a portion of a scan or a texture fill, as shown in Figure 7.3.

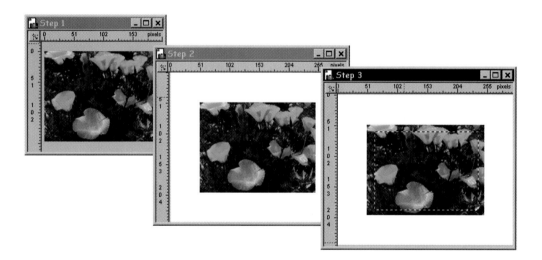

Figure 7.3 Creating an interesting edge in PhotoPaint

2 Set the paper color to white. Apply **Image/Paper Size**, deselecting the **Maintain Aspect Ratio** checkbox, and using a width of 300 pixels, a height of 250 pixels.

3 Using the Rectangle Mask tool, create a mask that is a little smaller than the image.

4 Select **Mask/Invert**. The mask will protect the image from the filter you will use in the next step, as shown in Figure 7.4.

You may want to use Image/Duplicate at this point, if you want to try some of the recipe variations on this same file later. You can save the file as a tif or cpt file at this point, and the mask will remain intact.

Figure 7.4 Applying a filter to create an interesting edge

5 Apply **Effects/Artistic/Vignette**; Vignette Mode, **White**; Offset, 0; Fade, 50.

RECIPES FOR EDGES IN PHOTOSHOP

Note: All of the following recipes start at step 4 as described in the example earlier in this chapter, by making a rectangular selection, then applying **Select/Invert**.

 Apply **Filter/Distort/Zigzag**; Amount, **13**; Ridges, **7**; Mode, **Pond Ripples**.

 Apply **Filter/Stylize/Diffuse**.

 Apply **Filter/Stylize/Find Edges**. Next, apply **Filter/Blur/Gaussian Blur** at **2** pixels.

 Set the background color to **white**. Apply **Filter/Stylize/Tiles**; Number of Tiles, **10**; Maximum Offset, **10%**; **Fill Empty Areas with Background Color**.

 Apply **Filter/Stylize/Wind**; Method, **Wind**; Direction, **Left**. Apply **Filter/Stylize/Wind**; Method, **Wind**; Direction, **Right**.

 Apply **Filter/Distort/Pinch**; Amount, **40%**.

Apply **Filter/Blur/Radial Blur**; Amount, **15**; Blur Method, **Spin**; Quality, **Good**.

Apply **Filter/Noise/Dust and Scratches**; Radius, **10**; Threshold, **0**.

Apply **Filter/Pixelate/Pointillize**; Cell Size, **5**. You may want to clean up the white area, which also becomes pointillized. Bucket fill the area with white.

Apply **Filter/Pixelate/Crystallize**, Cell Size, **5**.

Apply **Filter/Pixelate/Fragment**. Apply **Filter/Last Filter** (or **Ctrl+F**).

Apply **Filter/Stylize/Extrude**; Type, **Pyramids**; Size, **5**; Depth, **30**; **Random**; **Mask Incomplete Blocks**.

Photoshop

RECIPES FOR EDGES IN PHOTOPAINT

Note: All of the following recipes start at step 4 as described in the example earlier in this chapter.

Apply **Effects/2D/Pixelate**; **Circular**; Width, **4**; Height, **4**; Opacity, **80%**.

Apply **Effects/2D/ripple**; Direction, **Horizontal**; **Distort Ripple**; Period, **13**; Amplitude, **20**; Direction Angle, **45**. Next, apply **Effects/Blur/Soften**, at **40%**.

Select **Image/Flip/Vertically**. Apply **Effects/2D/Wet Paint**; Percentage, **80**; Wetness, **45**. Select **Image/Flip/Vertically** again. Apply **Effects/Last Filter** (or **Ctrl+F**).

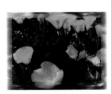

Apply **Image/Flip/Horizontally**. Apply **Effects/2D/Wind**; Opacity, **75**, Strength, **50**. Apply **Image/Flip/Horizontally** a second time to restore the image to its original position. Apply **Effects/Last Filter** (or **Ctrl+F**).

Apply **Effects/3D/Mesh Warp**. Pull in the center nodes for the desired warp. You may need to experiment a few times with the controls. Next, apply **Effects/Adjust/Color Tone Control**; Step, **30**; **Lighter**.

Apply **Effects/3D/Whirlpool**; Style, **Smudger**; Spacing, **18**; Smear Length, **10**; Twist, **45**; Streak Detail, **10**. Next, apply **Effects/Adjust/Color Tone Control**; Step, **10**; **Lighter**.

Apply **Effects/3D/Zigzag**; Period, **15**; Strength, **12**; Damping, **60**. Next, apply **Effects/Adjust/Color Tone Control**; Step, **30**; **Lighter**.

Apply **Effects/Artistic/Alchemy**. Select the **Color** tab, and change the background color to **White**. Select **Style**, **Cubist** and apply.

Apply **Effects/Artistic/Alchemy**. Select **Style**, **Oil Canvas Blur**. Next, apply **Effects/Adjust/Color Tone Control**; Step, **10**; **Lighter**.

Apply **Effects/Noise/Maximum**; Percentage, **60**; Radius, **4**.

Apply **Effects/Noise/Diffuse**; Level, **175**; select **Shuffle Edge Pixels**.

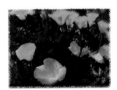

Apply **Effects/Render/Julia Set Explorer**. Select **Corel Presets/Rings of Saturn**. Select **Options/Lighten Only**, and deselect **Draw Gradient Across Top**.

PhotoPaint

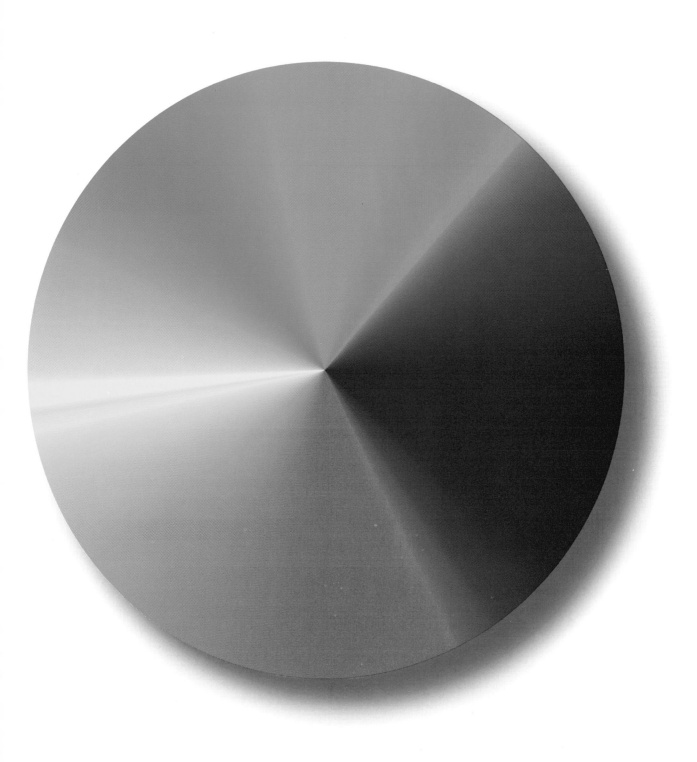

INDEXING COLORS AND CREATING TRANSPARENT GIFS, OR 8 BITS IS ENOUGH

So, now you've learned how to create graphics for the Web. Are you done? Not quite. Now I will address the not-so-fun part of Web graphics—file formats and color indexing. But this gives me an opportunity to explain transparency.

There are two basic file formats for web graphics, gif and jpeg. Gif is a compressed file format that allows a maximum of 256 colors in any image. Jpeg is also a compressed file format that allows the total spectrum, or 16 million colors, in any image. Understanding how and when to use gif and jpeg files, and learning how to use transparency will help you to create better looking, faster loading web graphics. Further, you will learn how to decrease the file size of gifs by indexing, or limiting the available colors to a specific palette.

After you get through these tasks, in Chapter Nine, I'll turn you into a guaranteed graphics genius by discovering how to create drop shadows. Meanwhile, back to indexing and transparency.

GIF VS. JPEG: LEARNING ABOUT INDEXING

In general, the two main file formats for use on the Web are gif and jpeg files. A gif file is an 8-bit (or less) graphics standard. The jpeg is a 24-bit compression standard. The more bits you have, the more precise information you have in your file. Both file formats are considered "lossy" compression methods; that is, information is lost in the compression process. It's a good idea to always keep a copy of the original, uncompressed, 24-bit file for this reason.

Only gif files are indexed, or constrained to a set of colors. If a file being indexed contains more than 256 colors, the missing colors are created by dithering, or approximating the missing color by using pixels of colors that are close in value. More colors in the original image, and the fewer colors in the Indexing palette creates a great deal of dithering.

If a monitor has a 256-color display, it can only display a maximum of 256 colors at any time. In Windows, 20 colors are reserved for the Windows System palette, and the other 236 colors are flexible. I've heard a lot of advice that you should index all of the images that will appear on the same web page to the identical 256-color (8-bit) palette. If images are indexed to the same palette, they will all contain the same 256 colors. Again, in theory, this means that less dithering will occur for monitors displaying (256) 8-bit color. I've done some testing, and this simply doesn't hold true. Your best bet is to always index the colors in your images to an adaptive palette. When images are indexed to an adaptive palette, the best 256 colors (or less) for that image are chosen.

Indexing isn't an issue for jpeg images, however. The rules of thumb for deciding between gif and jpeg formats are:

Use jpeg if your image is a photo or an illustration with many colors or smooth gradations of color. For example, a photograph often has a large amount of color variation that will be handled best by .jpg.

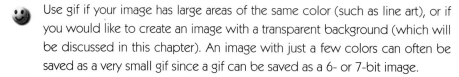
Use gif if your image has large areas of the same color (such as line art), or if you would like to create an image with a transparent background (which will be discussed in this chapter). An image with just a few colors can often be saved as a very small gif since a gif can be saved as a 6- or 7-bit image.

The first example, Figure 8.1, is a 57K jpeg file, saved with the medium quality setting. Actually it looks better on a monitor than Figure 8.2, which is a 72K gif file. The gif file was saved as a 4 bit (16 color) gif file.

I encourage you to experiment with saving your images in several different formats in order to compare the file sizes and appearance of your image.

Figure 8.1 This image is a 57K jpeg file.

Figure 8.2 This Image is a 72K gif file.

PhotoPaint has the drawback of not being able to save in an Indexed mode of less than 256 colors. The option to save as a 4-bit file is there, but it uses the standard Windows 16 colors for this format, and not colors from your image. If you want to save a file with less than 256 colors and you are using PhotoPaint, you'll want to use a shareware package, for example, LView Pro. Refer to the end of the chapter for a description of other options.

A Checklist for Creating Smaller Files

The following guidelines are helpful for creating smaller files:

1 Use gif and jpeg appropriately.

- Use jpeg if your image is a photo or an illustration with smooth gradations of color;

- Use gif if your image has large areas of the same color or if you would like to have a transparent background or if you want the image interlaced.

2 Experiment with different color depths when saving gifs. Most images can be saved in 6- or 7-bit format without much loss of quality.

3 If you need to resize a gif, change the color back to RGB before you resample. Index the colors again after you've resampled. This won't create a smaller file size, but it will create a less jaggy image.

4 It's rare that an image needs to be wider than 580 pixels. Truly. If you think that you need to tell people to set their browsers to a certain size, you're not really designing for the web.

5 Consider using an image in more than one place on a page. (Most browsers won't need to load the same graphic a second time.)

6 If you have a web page with many images, consider using thumbnails, or smaller versions of the images, that act as buttons linking to the larger images.

7 To dither or not to dither the gif? You can do both. I call this the Frankenstein method of image creation. The idea is to save the best parts of a dithered and nondithered version of the same image.

Figure 8.3 Image indexed without dithering.

Figure 8.4 Image indexed with dithering.

Before you index the colors in your image, duplicate it. Save one image with no dithering (Figure 8.3) and one image as dithered (Figure 8.4). Cut and paste the parts that look best into a single image. In figure 8.5 the undithered scissors were cut and pasted on top of the dithered background. Resave!

Figure 8.5 A hybrid of a dithered and nondithered image.

Interlacing Has Nothing to Do with Shoes

Interlacing is a nifty trick that you can apply to gifs, especially larger gifs. While the browser is loading up the web page, interlaced gifs will show up immediately at a very low resolution. As the browser continues to receive the rest of the gif, it rewrites the gif until the gif is completely rendered. This gives the illusion that the graphic is being received quickly. In reality, gifs saved as interlaced are, on average, about 10% larger than gifs saved as noninterlaced.

The only problem that can occur with interlaced gifs is that sometimes they fail to render completely, leaving a lower resolution image than intended. This can usually be corrected by using the browser's **Reload** command.

If a gif will be used as a background pattern for a page, it shouldn't be interlaced. Using an interlaced gif as a background tile will prevent the page from loading until the background gif is fully interlaced.

There are two flavors of gifs, gif 87a and gif 89a. Catchy names, right? You will want to use gif89a to use transparency or interlacing. Gif89a can be saved as either interlaced or noninterlaced files. Gif87a cannot be saved as interlaced or transparent files.

TRANSPARENCY

As you may know, bitmap files are geometrically challenged. A gif or any other bitmap can only be a rectangle. Transparency allows you to integrate your bitmaps seamlessly with the background of your web page. In other words, your round logo will not appear to be placed on a rectangular background, as shown in Figures 8.6 and 8.7.

Figure 8.6 Nontransparent background.

Figure 8.7 Transparent background.

Transparent backgrounds can be produced in a number of ways. Photoshop has a plug-in export filter (available at http://www.adobe.com/) for setting the transparent background, and PhotoPaint has a transparency option built into the **Save as Gif** function. The last part of this chapter discusses some shareware solutions to creating transparent backgrounds.

Be aware that a few potential problems can arise when creating transparent gifs. Only one color can be defined as transparent in any gif. If your background has been dithered to more than one color in the indexing process, you can end up with an ugly spotted mess since only the one color will be transparent. Another transparency problem can occur when the color that you have made transparent is used in places *other* than the background, causing the background to appear in unseemly (no pun intended) areas. The eyeball illustration in Figures 8.8 and 8.9 is the sad carrier of both of these gif problems.

Figure 8.8 The original image.

Figure 8.9 One color made transparent.

Fortunately, both of these problems can be corrected. If you're using the Gif89a filter from Adobe, running under Photoshop, you can avoid this entirely by defining which areas will become transparent before you apply the Gif89a filter. Open the **Windows/Palettes/Show Layers**, and use the flyout on the Layers palette to select **Duplicate Layer**. Turn off the eye icon for the Background Layer. Using whichever selection tool is appropriate, select the areas of your image that you want to make transparent. Select **Edit/Cut**, or use **Ctrl+X**. Apply **Export/Gif89a**. Export to finish. Yes, really, that's all.

If you're not using the Gif89a filter, you'll need to either bucket fill the problem area, or use a very small pencil or brush to retouch the dithered areas. This is single pixel tweaking time, but it's worth the effort to avoid creating a gif that is unattractive. I've found that it helps, when doing tedious work like cleaning up gifs, to put on some music.

In PhotoPaint, begin by converting your image to 256 colors by applying **Image/Convert to/256 Colors**, or by opening a saved gif file. Next, use the Eyedropper tool to select the color you wish to make transparent. Make a note of the Index number shown on the status bar. Select **File/Save As**. Select **Save As File Type**, **Gif**. A dialog box will open. Select **89a Format**, **Transparent**, and enter the Index number you recorded earlier.

Limitations of Browsers

Hey, what about those browsers that don't support background colors or transparency? Ready for a philosophy lesson? No, not about Plato, but about potential audiences. It is a fact that not all browsers are the same, nor are monitors and computers. While it's good practice to check how your images display on as many monitors and browsers as you can, you have no control over the way in which the users' browsers or monitors will dither or display your colors.

So, what does this mean to you? It means that there are problems that can occur due to the limitations of some monitors and browsers, and you can either decide to accommodate for those, or choose to go your own way and aim for just the way you want your page to look under optimum conditions.

I'll bet you were hoping that I would offer the definitive answer. As long as there are so many different browsers and monitors out there, the decision is up to you.

Creating Transparent GIFs: Step-by-Step Instructions

Some of the most common shareware used to create transparent gifs includes GIF Construction Set, GiFTrans, LView Pro, and Paint Shop Pro 3.11. the following sections offer step-by-step instructions for creating transparent gifs.

GIF Construction Set

GIF Construction Set for Windows will allow you to create transparent gifs and it supports interlacing. You can also load a palette from one gif and apply it to other gifs with GIF Construction Set.

To create a transparent GIF with GIF construction set, open your gif file (GIF Construction set will not open formats other than gif), use the Insert/Control icons. Then, from the button bar, select **Edit**. From the Edit menu, check the **Transparent Colour** checkbox. To the right of the checkbox is a color swatch. Click on the color swatch to view the gif's palette and select the color that you wish to make transparent as shown in Figure 8.10. Click on the **View** icon. The color you have chosen to be transparent will be masked with dark gray.

To make a gif interlaced, open your gif file. Highlight the Image line, and select **Edit** from the button bar. From the Edit menu, check the **Interlaced** checkbox. From this menu you can also save and load indexed color palettes.

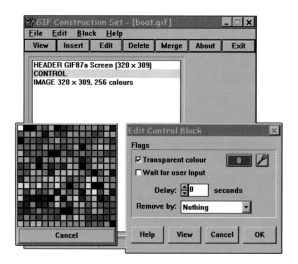

Figure 8.10 Using Gif Construction Set

GiFTrans

GiFTrans is a DOS command-line program to create transparent gifs. You need to know the hex code (see Chapter Five) of the color you want to make transparent first. Then, at the DOS command line, you would type

```
giftrans -t #000000 - newfile.gif file.gif
```

In the above example, the number following the **#** symbol would be your hex color code, the **newfile.gif** would be the name of the file after it has been made transparent, and **file.gif** is the name of your original file. This is not for the DOS-impaired user.

LView Pro

There are five versions of LView Pro. You want to use version 1.C, 32-bit, or later.

To make a transparent background with LView Pro, open your gif file. Then choose **File/Options/Background Color**. The Select Color Palette Entry dialog box will open, allowing you to choose the color you would like to make transparent. Select the **eyedropper** icon and use the Eyedropper tool to select the color of the area you want to make transparent. Select the **Mask Selection Using** checkbox. LView will mask out the areas of your gif that will not be transparent with either black or white. This is the reverse of how most gif utilities work.

Paint Shop Pro 3.11

Version 3.1 creates transparent and interlaced gifs. Paint Shop Pro is also a very nice shareware paint package with many capabilities you would expect only from higher end commercial paint packages. The only drawback to using Paint Shop Pro to create transparent gifs is that you can't preview which area of your gif is being made transparent. You can work on a gif that is already transparent and save the gif with its original transparency.

To make a transparent gif in Paint Shop Pro, you need to first reduce the color depth. Go to **Colors/Decrease Color Depth/X Colors**. You can select the number of colors that you would like to reduce your gif to. For the method of color reduction, choose **Error Diffusion**. This will dither your image when reducing your colors.

Zoom in on your image to make sure that your background color hasn't become dithered. If it has, use the Paintbucket tool to fill the background with a single color, or use a paintbrush or pencil to eliminate colors from the background. Once your background is a single color, use the Eyedropper tool to select it, as shown in Figure 8.11. At the bottom edge of the window, Paint Shop Pro will display the index number. This is the number in the image's palette that you'll make transparent.

Figure 8.11 Using Paint Shop Pro

Select **Save As**. The file type should be gif 89A. Select the **Options** button. Select **Override Image's Settings/Enable Transparency/Use Specific Index**. The number you use for the index color is the number displayed when you used the Eyedropper tool.

Part 3: Advanced Web Topics

Chapter 9

CREATING FLOATING TYPE, OR THE SHADOW KNOWS

HTML doesn't allow a great deal of control over how type appears on a web page. Using type within a graphic allows you complete freedom to use any typeface in any style, color or combination that you like. One of the great things about working with type is that once you learn a few basics, such as how to create a drop shadow, you can make very professional looking artwork fairly easily.

There are a few basic things to know about working with type. First, type needs to be legible, so the more complex the typeface you're working with, the larger it should be. If you're working at a very small size, you will probably want to select a simple sans serif typeface, such as Arial or Futura. Serif typefaces tend to be a little more complex, and thus more difficult to make out at smaller sizes.

If you use a purposely degraded font (like a grunge font) at a small point size as in Figure 9.1, instead of appearing intentionally rough it will just look unclear and poorly anti-aliased. Using a large point size along with a drop shadow can help clarify your intentions and the legibility of the type, as shown in Figure 9.2.

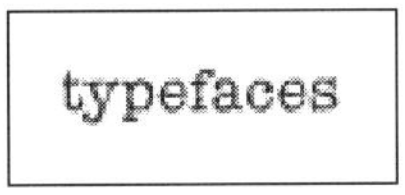

Figure 9.1 Type at a very small size

Figure 9.2 Type at a larger size

Also, to help keep the type legible, heighten the contrast between the type and its background. So, if you're using a dark color for the type, use a light color for the background and vice versa. You can also tweak the contrast by using the **Adjust Levels** command, as I discussed in Chapter Five. I'll be using bold or extra bold versions of typefaces in the examples to help the type stand out.

All of the projects and recipes that are included in this chapter can also be used with logos, symbols, or line art. Get creative and use some of the edge treatments from Chapter Seven on the finished graphic.

I'll start with two examples. The first is the ever-popular answer to the question, "How do I make a drop shadow?" The second project addresses creating type with a drop shadow on a transparent gif.

PHOTOSHOP: CREATING TYPE WITH A DROP SHADOW

1 Open a new file, 300x100 pixels. Open the Layers palette by selecting **Windows/Show Layers**.

2 Fill the Background Layer with a pattern fill that you created in Chapter Four. Open the pattern file you want to use, and **Select All** (or **Ctrl+A**) and apply **Edit/Define Pattern**. Return to the new image you're creating, and select **Edit/Fill/Pattern**; Opacity, **100%**; Mode, **Normal**.

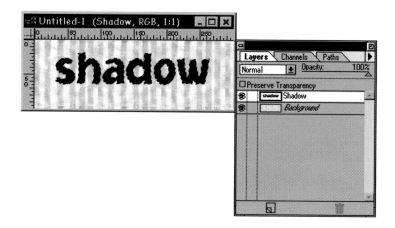

Figure 9.3 Creating a Shadow Layer

3 Create a new Layer by selecting **New Layer** from the flyout menu on the Layers palette. Name the Layer "Shadow" (see Figure 9.3). Select **black** as the foreground color, and click the **Text** tool on your image. Type "shadow" at about 40 points using a bold or extra bold typeface. I'm sure that by now you know that this will be anti-aliased.

4 Copy the type by using **Ctrl+C**. Apply **Edit/Paste Layer**. Name the layer *Type* (see Figure 9.4).

Figure 9.4 Creating the Type Layer

5 Select all of the nontransparent pixels on the Type Layer by using **Ctrl+Alt+T**. At this point, you can apply any type of fill that you want to the type, including a gradient or texture fill.

Select **red** for the foreground color and **burgundy** as the background color. Drag the Gradient tool from the top to the bottom of the image. If you want to constrain the gradient to a precisely angled fill, use the **Ctrl** key in conjunction with the Gradient tool.

Use **Ctrl+D** to deselect the type, as shown in Figure 9.5.

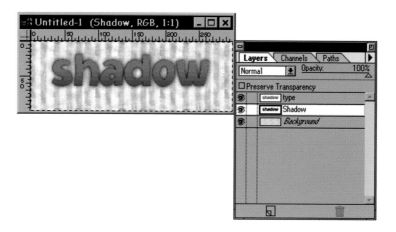

Figure 9.5 Blurring the Type Layer

6 Select the **Shadow Layer**. Apply **Filter/Blur/Gaussian Blur** at **2** pixels. You can offset the shadow by using **Ctrl+A** to select the shadow, and then nudge the shadow down and to the right using the arrow keys on your keypad.

At the top of the Layers palette, you'll see an opacity slider. Slide the opacity slider until the shadow looks good, somewhere around 80%. Lessening the opacity of the shadow allows some of the background to show through (Figure 9.6), makes the shadow look more natural and less like it was painted on the background.

Figure 9.6 Type with a drop shadow

7 Using the flyout menu from the Layers palette, select **Flatten**. Save the file as a medium quality jpg file.

PHOTOSHOP: CREATING TYPE WITH A TRANSPARENT BACKGROUND

Thanks to the Gif89a export filter, and the fact that the type and its shadow are created on separate layers, creating type with a transparent background in Photoshop is a fairly easy task.

You're going to repeat the preceding steps 1 through 6, with one exception. Start with a file 300x100 pixels, but do not fill the background layer. Instead, turn off the background layer by toggling the **eye** icon for the background layer (see Figure 9.7).

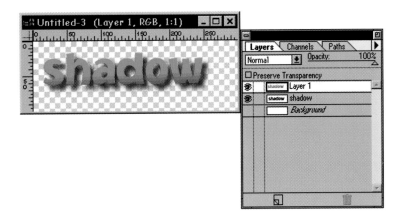

Figure 9.7 The Background layer turned off

Then, find the RGB value for the color you will be using as a background on your web page. Do this by using the Eyedropper tool to select the color, which will also make the color the foreground color. Then, double-click on the **Foreground Color** swatch to find the RGB value.

7 Apply **File/Export/Gif89a**. Select the number of colors you would like to index the image to. Click on the **Transparency Index Color** swatch, and enter the RGB value for the transparent color. For this example, the Transparency Index Color was set to a **pale pink**, as shown in Figure 9.8.

Figure 9.8 Image saved with a pink background

CREATING TYPE WITH A DROP SHADOW IN PHOTOPAINT

1 Open a new file 300x100 pixels. Open the Objects roll-up by selecting **View/Roll-ups/Objects**.

2 Fill the background with a pattern that you created in Chapter Four by double-clicking on the **Fill** tool to open the Fill roll-up. Select **Bitmap Fill/Edit/Import**. Select the tile you want to use. Fill the background with the Fill tool (Figure 9.9).

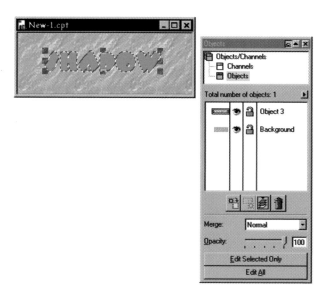

Figure 9.9 Creating the Type

3 Select **red** as the paint color. Click the **Text** tool on the image, and type 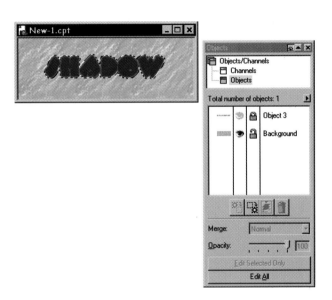 the word "shadow." Use a bold typeface at about 40 points. Of course, you don't want to forget the anti-aliasing. Select **Mask/Create from Object**. Select **Mask/Feather**; **5** pixels; Edges, **Soft**; Direction, **Outside** (Figure 9.10).

Figure 9.10 Creating the shadow mask

4 Make the Type object invisible by turning off the **eye** icon. Select the **Fill** tool, and set the fill transparency to **30**. (Remember to change the transparency back to its default, **0** for the next time you use the Fill roll-up). Fill the feathered mask you've created with black (Figure 9.11).

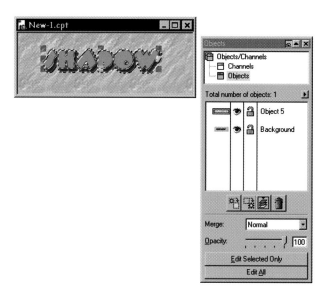

Figure 9.11 Filling the shadow mask

5 Select the **Type object** on the Object roll-up to make it visible again. Use the arrow keys to nudge the type up and to the left, so that it is offset from the shadow (Figure 9.12). Select **Object/Combine/All Objects with Background**. Save the file as a jpg.

Figure 9.12 Type with a drop shadow

PhotoPaint: Creating Type with a Transparent Background

The steps for creating type on a transparent background would be the same steps that you followed for the first example, except that instead of using a pattern fill for step 2, you will want to fill the background with the same color that the web page will be, as shown in Figure 9.13.

Figure 9.13 Saving with a transparent background

After you follow the steps to create the shadow and the type, you'll need to select **Image/Convert To/256 Colors/Adaptive, Error Diffusion**. Then, once the colors are indexed, find out what the Index Number is for the background color by using the **Eyedropper** tool to select the background color, and looking for the Index Number on the status line.

Then, apply **Save As Gif**, using 89A Format, Transparent Color. Enter the **Index Number** for the color you wish to make transparent, and you're finished.

TYPE RECIPES FOR PHOTOSHOP

Note: All of the recipes are 300x100 pixels in size, and follow the directions for the example in the chapter with exceptions noted.

Follow the directions for type with a drop shadow, using a white fill for the Background Layer, and magenta for the Shadow Layer. Blur the Shadow Layer by applying **Filter/Blur/Gaussian Blur**, **3** pixels. On the Type Layer, fill the type with white. Do not offset the blur as we did in the example earlier in the chapter.

Start with three layers. The Background Layer will be filled with white. Add two new layers, *Type* and *Texture*. The Texture Layer will be on top. Select the **Texture Layer**, fill with a **dark red**, and apply **Filter/Noise/Add Noise**. Select the **Type Layer**, and select **black** as the foreground color. Type "Cut Out." Without deselecting the type shape, select the **Texture Layer**. Apply **Ctrl+X** to cut the type shape out of the Type Layer. You will be able to see the Type Layer through the hole you just cut out in the Texture Layer. Return to the Type Layer, and set the Opacity slider to **60**. Use **Ctrl+A** and the arrow keys to nudge the type up and to the left. Finish by deselecting the type and applying **Filter/Blur/Gaussian Blur** at **2** pixels.

Create type with a drop shadow, as described earlier in this chapter. Flatten the image, then select **Filter/Render/Lighting**. Use the Default Spotlight, set the Texture Channel to **Blue**, and change the Height to **60**.

Create type with a drop shadow as described earlier in this chapter. Select the **Type Shape** on the Type Layer by applying **Ctrl+Alt+T**. Open a photo (I used the colorized photo of Yosemite from Chapter Six). Select an area you want to use and copy it to the clipboard using **Ctrl+C**. Return to the type image, and select **Edit/Paste Into**.

This example only requires two Layers: the *Background Layer* and the *Type Layer*. Fill the Background Layer with black. Select the **Type Layer**, and make green the foreground color. Create the green type and deselect (**Ctrl+D**). Apply **Filter/Blur/Gaussian Blur** at **2** pixels.

Fill the Background Layer with gray, and create type with a drop shadow as described earlier in this chapter. Select the **type** on the Type Layer by using **Ctrl+Alt+T**. Change the foreground color to dark gray and the background color to medium gray. Fill the type on the Type Layer with a gray linear gradient using the Gradient tool.

Fill the Background Layer with **black**. Select the **Shadow Layer**, and make **red** the foreground color. Create the red type and deselect (**Ctrl+D**). Apply **Filter/Blur/Gaussian Blur** at **3** pixels. Select the **Type Layer** and again add red type. Do not deselect the type, instead, apply **Select/Modify/Contract** at **2** pixels. Apply **Select/Feather** at **2** pixels, and fill the resulting selection with **white**.

Fill the Background Layer with a texture fill. On the Shadow Layer, add the type but don't blur. Set the Opacity on the Shadow Layer to **50%**. Use white for the type on the Type Layer, then apply **Filter/Stylize Emboss**; Angle, **50**; Height, **2** pixels; Amount, **100%**. Change the Layer mode of the Type Layer to **Soft Light**.

Apply **Filter/Noise/Add Noise** to the Background Layer, then apply **Filter/Stylize Emboss**; Angle, **50**; Height, **2** pixels; Amount, **100%**. On the Shadow Layer, fill the type with a black to dark gray gradient, then apply **Filter/Blur/Gaussian Blur** at **2** pixels. Select **Image/Effects/Skew**, and drag the upper-right handle to the right of the image. Use white for the type on the Type Layer.

Select **medium blue** as the foreground color and **dark blue** as the background color. Select the **Background Layer** and apply **Filter/Render/ Clouds**. Select the **type** and add the type, using white for the fill. Apply **Filter/Stylize Emboss**; Angle, **50**; Height, **2** pixels; Amount, **100%**. Select the **Type Layer** and use dark blue instead of black for the type on the Shadow Layer. Apply **Filter/Blur/Gaussian Blur** at **3** pixels.

TYPE RECIPES FOR PHOTOPAINT

Note: All of the recipes are 300x100 pixels in size and follow the directions for the example in the chapter with exceptions noted.

Create the type at about 48 points, using white for the Paint Color. Select **Mask/Create** from Object. Toggle off the type Object by selecting the **eye** icon so that you can see the mask you've created. Fill the mask with gray. Select **Mask/None**, and apply **Effects/Blur/Gaussian Blur** at **2** pixels. Toggle the type Object back on, and fill with a Bitmap fill. Select **Object/Combine/All Objects with Background**, and save the file.

Fill the background with light blue. Create the type at about 48 points. Select **Mask/Create from Object**. Delete the type Object by selecting the **garbage can** icon. Fill the mask with a dark blue. Apply **Mask/Feather**; Size, **1** pixel; Direction, **Outside**; Edges, **Soft**. Apply **Effects/3D/The Boss**; Width, **5** pixels; Height, **10** pixels; Drop Off, **Flat**.

Create the type at about 48 points, using white for the Paint Color. Select **Mask/Create from Object**. Toggle off the type Object by selecting the **eye** icon so that you can see the mask you've created. Apply **Mask/Feather**; Size, **3** pixels; Direction, **Outside**; Edges, **Soft**. Fill the mask with dark blue. Select **Mask/None**, and apply **Effects/Blur/Gaussian Blur** at **3** pixels. Toggle the type Object back on. Select **Object/Combine/All Objects with Background**, and save the file.

PhotoPaint

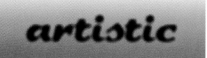

Fill the background with a dark orange to pale yellow gradient, using the **Fountain Fill** option from the Fill roll-up, set to a 90° angle. Create the type at about 48 points, using white for the Paint Color. Select **Mask/Create from Object**. Toggle off the type Object by selecting the **eye** icon so that you can see the mask you've created. Fill the mask with dark brown. Select **Mask/None**, and apply **Effects/Blur/Gaussian Blur** at **3** pixels. Toggle the type Object back on.

Fill the type with the same gradient fill, with the angle set to **-90**. Select **Object/Combine/All Objects with Background**, and save the file.

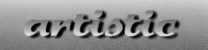

Create the type at about 48 points. Select **Mask/Create from Object**. Delete the type Object by selecting the **garbage can** icon. Fill the mask with a dark blue. Set the current fill to **light blue**. Apply **Select/Feather**; Size, **1** pixel; Direction, **Outside**; Edges, **Soft**. Apply **Effects/3D/Glass**; Style, **Warp**; Bevel Width, **4**; **Drop Off**; **Flat**; Color, **Foreground**.

Fill the background with pale violet. Create the type at about 48 points. Select **Mask/Create from Object**. Delete the type Object by selecting the garbage can icon. Apply **Mask/Feather**; Size, **1** pixel; Direction, **Outside**; Edges, **Soft**. Fill the mask with purple. Apply **Effects/3D/Emboss**; Emboss Color, **Original**; Depth, **2**.

Fill the background with a Bitmap Fill. Create the type at about 48 points, using white for the Paint Color. Select **Mask/Create from Object**. Delete the type Object by selecting the **garbage can** icon. Fill the mask with white. Apply **Effects/Color**

Adjust/Brightness-Contrast-Intensity; Brightness, **73**. Select **Mask/Invert**. Select the **paintbrush** tool, and select **Airbrush**; **Multiply**; Size, **30**, and paint behind the text.

Fill the background with a Texture Fill. The fill used in this recipe was from the Texture Library, Samples 6; Texture List, Cobwebs. Create the type at about 48 points, using black for the Paint Color. Copy the type Object by using **Crl+C**. Select **Edit/Paste/As New Object**. Using the object Tool Settings roll-up, set the Object Scale to **Horizontal, 100; Vertical, 100**; and depress the **vertical mirror** icon. This will flip the type vertically. Set the opacity for the type copy Object, using the slider at the bottom of the Objects menu, to **40%**. Select **Object/Combine/All Objects with Background** and save the file.

Fill the background with pale blue to white linear gradient. Create the type at about 48 points, using dark blue. Select **Mask/Create from Object**. Toggle off the type Object by selecting the **eye** icon. Fill the mask with dark blue. Select **Mask/None**. Apply **Effects/Blur/Gaussian Blur** at **2** pixels. Toggle the type Object back on, and drag to offset from the shadow. Select **Object/Combine/All Objects with Background**. Select **Mask/All**. Apply **Effects/3D/ 3D Rotate; Best Fit; Vertical, 10**.

Fill the background with black. Create the type at about 48 points, using a pale green. Select **Object/ Combine/ All Objects with Background**. Select **Effects/Blur/Gaussian Blur** at **2** pixels.

PhotoPaint

CHAPTER TEN

IMPORTING AND EXPORTING OR LITTLE WHITE LINES SERRATED EDGES, AND OTHER AMUSEMENTS

The only thing constant in life is change. At some point, you'll need to convert files from different file formats to gif or jpeg for the web. Hopefully, the files you'll be using won't be in some rare format that existed for only three months in 1982 within a proprietary graphics package now impossible to find.

In this chapter I'll discuss importing vector files, and importing bitmap files, along with different strategies for each. A file has to be in a bitmap format (jpeg or gif) in order to display on a Web page. For many reasons, you may start out with a vector file and export it as a bitmap as one of the final steps. I will discuss strategies for working with vector and bitmap files so that they yield the highest quality image for your website.

WELCOME TO PLANET VECTOR

Vector based files are object based, with the objects made up of mathematically defined lines and shapes. Common vector-based applications are CorelDRAW, Illustrator, Canvas, or Freehand. Type is also vector based. Common vector-based file formats include cdr (CorelDRAW), eps (Encapsulated Post Script), and ai (Adobe Illustrator).

Bitmap files are made up of individual pixels. Paint programs, such as Photoshop, PhotoPaint, Painter, Matisse, and xRes, use bitmap file formats. Common bitmap file formats include bmp, tif, gif, jpeg, and pct.

So what's the difference, really, between vector and bitmap? Vector-based objects can be easily manipulated independently of one another. Vector objects can be resized, rotated, and rescaled without a loss of quality. Bitmapped objects have to be manipulated on the pixel level, and they degrade in quality each time they are rotated, skewed or resampled.

In Figures 10.1 and 10.2, you can see that when the blue rectangle object is deleted, it does not affect the two other objects. If the artwork had been created in a bitmap program, the blue rectangle could only have been removed by creating a selection, and then deleting it.

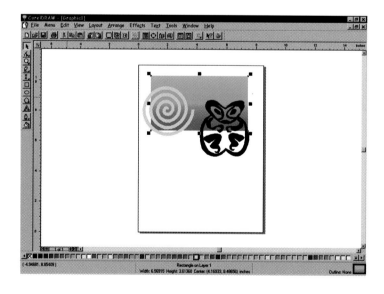

Figure 10.1 Three objects in CorelDRAW

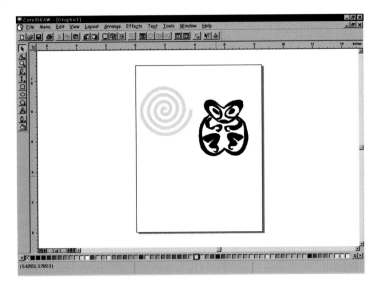

Figure 10.2 One object removed

Vector-based artwork offers a great deal of flexibility, yet working in a paint program allows you to control the positioning, size, and texture of your artwork at the pixel level.

There once was a much clearer dividing line between what was vector based and what was bitmap based. But with each new revision of software, paint programs become more vector-like, employing strategies such as Layers (in Photoshop) or Objects (in PhotoPaint) to allow you to manipulate portions of the bitmap you're creating independently. Drawing programs have become much more bitmap oriented, too, including tools such as the bitmap fills, or the Bitmap Lens Effects in CorelDRAW.

If you'll be using the same image at many different resolutions, it is usually best to start with a vector-based file. If, for instance, you have a logo that will appear at a size of 20x20 pixels on one page, and 200x200 pixels on another, and 100x100 pixels on a third page, it makes sense to create the logo as a vector-based file, and import it to the size you need.

If you are working on artwork that won't need to be resized, the best strategy might be to create the image in your paint program, using Layers or Objects to control different parts of your artwork independently of one another.

FROM PLANET VECTOR TO PHOTOSHOP

How do you make the leap from vector to bitmap? First, export your vector file as an ai or eps file. To do this from within CorelDRAW, first select your logo on the page, then you'll want to select **File/Export**, **Adobe Illustrator ai/eps format**, and **Selected Only**. You'll then see the dialog box shown in Figure 10.3.

Figure 10.3 Adobe Illustrator Export dialog box

You'll want to select **Adobe Illustrator 3.0** as the Format, and **Export Text as Curves**.

Next, open Photoshop, and select **File/Open/Filename**. You'll receive the Rasterize Adobe Illustrator Format dialog box. Make sure that the anti-aliased checkbox is selected (of course!), and that the mode is set to RGB Color (see Figure 10.4).

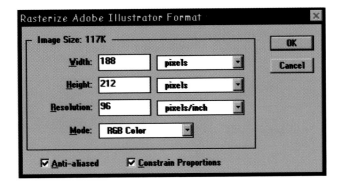

Figure 10.4 Importing an eps file into Photoshop

You can set the Width and Height to any size you wish, and the image will automatically have anti-aliased edges as long as the anti-aliased checkbox is selected, as shown in Figure 10.5.

Figure 10.5 The imported eps file

Your logo will open with a transparent background. You can then select **File/Export/Gif89a** to save the logo as a gif with a transparent background (see Figure 10.6).

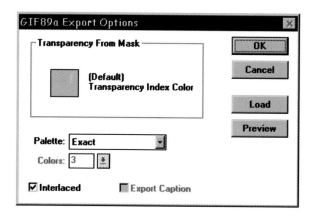

Figure 10.6 Exporting the file as a gif

There's another potential "gotcha" here. You can see that the palette reads **Exact**, and the Colors, **3**. If the edges are to appear anti-aliased for this logo, it will need more than three colors. Change the palette to **Adaptive**, and select the number of colors you wish to index to. You can change the Transparency Index Color to the color of the web page the logo will appear on. In Figure 10.7, the logo has been saved with a white background.

Figure 10.7 The finished artwork

FROM PLANET VECTOR TO PHOTOPAINT

Getting a vector-based file from Corel Draw to PhotoPaint is more flexible than it used to be. Once you've created your file in Draw, you can either export as a bitmapped file or open the CorelDRAW file from within PhotoPaint.

From within PhotoPaint, after you select **File/Open/filename.cdr**, you'll see the Import Into Bitmap dialog box. It's always a good idea to import using the highest color value possible. There are a plethora of choices under the Size dialog box. However, if you choose anything other than 1 to 1, your image will be squished horizontally or vertically to fit the dimensions you choose.

If you want to import at a size larger or smaller than the Width and Height specify, you can change the Size to **Custom**, and change the Width and Height amounts. You'll want to maintain the proportional values between the Width and Height.

You'll notice, too, that there is an anti-aliasing checkbox, which for this example I've checked (see Figure 10.8).

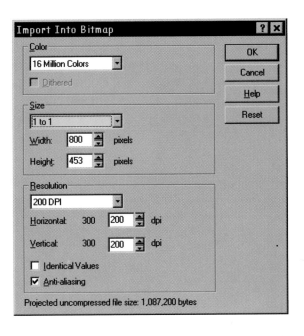

Figure 10.8 Import CDR dialog box in PhotoPaint

However, when the imported cdr file is opened as a bitmap, the spiral is anti-aliased, but the text included in the graphic isn't. What is going on in Figure 10.9?

Figure 10.9 The imported CDR file

It turns out that the anti-aliasing function only applies to objects that have had an outline specified in CorelDRAW.

Your second guess would probably be to export as a gif directly from within CorelDRAW. You can export your CorelDRAW graphic as a gif, and specify dithered color as well. However, you can't choose the type of dithering, and Corel uses a Pattern method of applying dither. The graphic on the left was exported as a 16-million-color tif from within CorelDRAW, opened in PhotoPaint, and indexed to 256-colors using an adaptive palette and an error diffusion setting. The image on the right was exported from CorelDRAW as a 256 color gif, with the **dither** checkbox selected. The best quality method of dithering when reducing an image to a gif file is attained using an adaptive palette with error diffusion, which creates transitions between colors by a diffused pattern of pixels. Exporting directly from CorelDRAW is done with a pattern type of dithering, which create a visually obvious, and less smooth, dithering as shown in Figure 10.10.

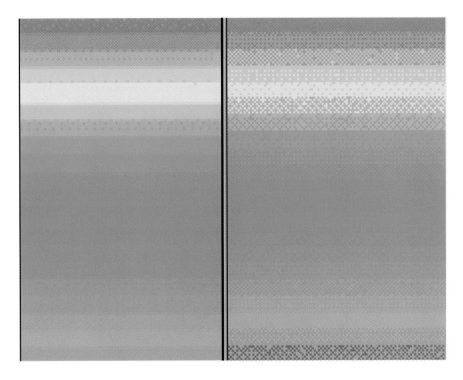

Figure 10.10 Two methods of dithering

It's almost as bad as algebra, trying to figure out what is the best way to get from CorelDRAW to a web page. Luckily, there is a reliable work around.

Open your cdr file from within PhotoPaint at a larger size than what you want to end up with. You can do this by first checking to see what the pixel values are for Height and Width when the Size setting is 1 to 1. Then change the Size setting to **Custom**, and enter in pixel values that are **150%** of the original values for Height and Width. Make sure you import at 16 million colors, and don't check the anti-aliasing checkbox.

Yes, you heard me right. Don't check the anti-aliasing checkbox on the Bitmap Import dialog box. Instead, once the image is imported, apply **Edit/Resample**, and enter the values you want to use for the final pixel size of your image. Make sure that the anti-aliasing checkbox is checked on the Resample dialog box.

Doing all of the anti-aliasing during resampling means that everything will be anti-aliased only once, and at the same level of consistency, as shown in Figure 10.11.

Figure 10.11 The anti-aliased gif

The latest version of CorelDRAW only partially fixes the little-white-lines-and-serrated-edges export problem that the previous versions of CorelDRAW were cursed with. Previous versions of the program always added a 1-pixel white border around any bitmap export, and 6.0 is the first version of CorelDRAW to offer anti-aliasing as an option to exports. It has been my experience that it's best to do any anti-aliasing or color reduction from within a paint program, and not through the Corel Export function.

THE MAC TO PC, AND PC TO MAC DANCE

"My computer can't read your disk."

I don't know of many things that can make me clench my teeth like that sentence. Maybe three: "The check is in the mail," or "I lost your invoice," or "I've never heard of that happening" (especially when it comes from software tech support). Honestly, it's usually not the files that are the problem. It's the darned disk.

Apple's latest operating system, System 7.5, will read PC disks without a problem. Earlier versions of the Mac operating system will need a software conversion program to recognize PC disks. If you're on the PC trying to read a Mac-formatted disk, you will need a software conversion program to be able to read Mac disks.

Thank goodness for modems. You can avoid the whole disk problem by attaching files to e-mail, or by FTPing the files to your website for the other person to download, or by FTPing directly to the other person's server.

As far as file formats go, gif, and jpeg, tif and pct bitmap files should be easily read on both platforms. I've also successfully traded the psd files, with Layers intact, across platforms. Additionally, I've had no problem exporting CorelDraw files as ai files.

TRULY UNUSUAL FILE FORMATS, AND WHAT TO DO WITH THEM

If you're stuck with an unusual file format that you need to convert for the web, there's a very useful piece of software called Image Alchemy. Image Alchemy will convert between dozens of file formats I've never even heard of before.

It is a DOS command-line program, but it will convert a whole directory of files at once if you want it to. It's definitely worth investigating if you have to convert rare file formats. You can visit the website of Handmade Software, creators of Image Alchemy, at http://www.handmadesw.com/.

CHAPTER
11

SPEEDING UP YOUR WORK WITHOUT CAFFEINE OR OTHER ARTIFICIAL STIMULANTS

Once you understand how to use the tools in a software program to achieve the effects you're looking for, there are really only two things that can stand in your way of enjoying your work. The first computer graphics killjoy is a lack of organization, and the second is mind-numbing repetitive work. Any project that you work on in Photoshop or PhotoPaint will have some repetition. Certain projects (like creating a series of seamless pattern tiles) will have a great deal of repetition.

First, I'll go through some strategies to cut down on some of the time-consuming aspects of repetitive work. In the second part of this chapter, I will discuss methods of organization.

SPEEDING UP REPETITIVE WORK IN PHOTOSHOP

By following the next two steps in Photoshop, you should be able to speed up your work considerably. First, learn some common key strokes. It will only take a few minutes, and I promise that you won't regret it. You will save hours and hours of time in the long run by learning some shortcuts right now.

Here are the keystrokes I use most often:

Ctrl+A	Select all
Ctrl+C	Copy
Ctrl+D	Deselect
Ctrl+H	Hide a Selection
Ctrl+S	Save
Ctrl+V	Paste
Ctrl+X	Cut (useful for Layers)
Ctrl+Z	Undo

The other thing to learn is how to use the **Shift**, **Control**, and **Alt** keys in conjunction with Photoshop tools. Take a few moments now and again to experiment with the using these keys with the tools. I know when someone is really comfortable using Photoshop if they use the keyboard as often as the mouse.

The second trick to help speed up your work is to edit the Command palette. "The what?" you ask. This way, please.

PHOTOSHOP: EDITING THE COMMAND PALETTE

1 From the menu bar, select **Window/Palette/Show** commands. The Command palette will pop up on your screen (see Figure 11.1), and you can have it visible at all times. Why is this the greatest thing since sliced bread? Well, if you have commands imprinted on your brain from other programs, you can change Photoshop's **Function** key assignments to match what you already know. You can also assign a color to each command, or a group of commands on your palette. It's also possible to save and load different palettes for different tasks.

Figure 11.1 The default Command palette

You can use the commands on the palette either by using their assigned Function key, or by just simply clicking on the command itself, as shown in Figure 11.2.

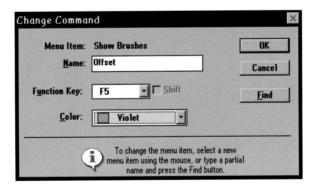

Figure 11.2 The Change Command dialog box

From the flyout menu, select **Edit Commands**. Select **Show Brushes/Change**. Change the **Show Brushes** command to the **Filter/Other/Offset Filter**. If you're not sure of the name of the command you want, you can select the **Find** button, or you can simply select the command you want to use from the main menu bar. Change the color to violet. Select **OK**.

3 Figure 11.3 shows how the Commands palette looks after the changes have been applied. Continue to change the commands to suit the way that you work. When you've finished applying all of the changes, from the flyout menu select **Save Commands** (see Figures 11.4 and 11.5). If the Options palette is not open, select **Windows/Show Options**. Drag the finished Commands palette onto the Options palette.

Figure 11.3 Editing the Command palette

Figure 11.4 The edited Command palette

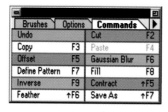

Figure 11.5 Adding the Command Palette to the Brushes

PHOTOPAINT: SPEEDING UP REPETITIVE WORK

The first thing to do in order to speed up your work is to take a few minutes to learn some of the most common keystrokes from PhotoPaint. Memorizing is no fun, but I can guarantee it will be worth every minute. As a bonus, the keystrokes that you use in PhotoPaint will also work in CorelDRAW, so you're really getting two shortcuts for the price of one.

Ctrl+C	**Copy**
Ctrl+N	**New File**
Ctrl+S	**Save**
Ctrl+V	**Paste**
Ctrl+X	**Cut (copies the cut portion to the clipboard)**
Ctrl+Z	**Undo**

You can change or customize keystrokes within PhotoPaint by applying **Tools/Customize/Keyboard**. Once again, if you have certain keystrokes that you've learned while using other programs, you can remap the shortcuts from within PhotoPaint to match what you already know.

CUSTOMIZING THE TOOLBAR IN PHOTOPAINT

I will show you how to customize the icon toolbar in PhotoPaint so that common tools are always available. It might be worth your time to analyze which tools and commands you use most frequently so that you can customize your toolbar to suit the way that you work.

1 Open a new document. You won't be doing anything with this document. Having a document open will allow us to customize the toolbars. Select **View/Toolbar**. Select **Standard and Toolbox**, and deselect any other toolbars.

2 You will now only have the standard toolbar visible at the top of the screen, as shown in Figure 11.6. The standard toolbar has a lot of icons for tools I rarely use. To delete icons from the toolbar, select the **icon**, and **Alt+Drag** the icon from the toolbar. To reposition the icons on the toolbar, **Alt+Drag** the icon into a new position.

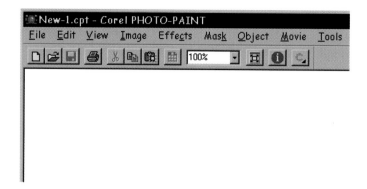

Figure 11.6 The PhotoPaint Toolbar

In Figure 11.7, I've deleted everything except for the icons for Cut, Paste as New Object, View, File Info, and Application Launcher.

Figure 11.7 The Standard Toolbar

3 It's time to go icon shopping! To add icons for other tools within PhotoPaint, select **Tools/Customize/Toolbars**. Go through the lists of tool icons. You can hold your mouse over any icon to view its title. When you find a useful tool, drag the icon to your toolbar, as shown in Figure 11.8.

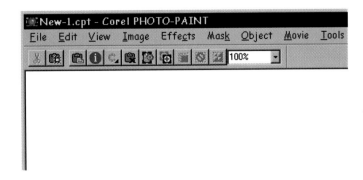

Figure 11.8 Editing the Toolbar

GETTING ORGANIZED AND LIVING HAPPILY EVER AFTER

Getting organized is the secret to a happy life. At least it seems that way if you've ever spent more than half an hour trying to find a file that you need to deliver to a client. I wish that I could say that I was naturally gifted in the area of organization, but, sadly, I've had to learn all of these organizing tricks the hard way.

Building a website means, generally, dealing with a lot of small files that are linked together and need to be updated very frequently. It means that being organized from the beginning can save you hours of time in the long run. Often there will be new revisions and slightly different versions of a file that you'll need to track. For instance, you might have a logo on a white background, a logo on a gray background, a logo on a button bar, and so on.

Following are some organizing tips that work for me. In the end, you have to find a method of tracking files and revisions that works best for you.

1 Keep all the files for the same project in one directory, broken down into sub-directories if necessary. I keep all the files for a client in a single directory. I keep a separate directory within each client's directory for uploads, so that I can keep track of what I have e-mailed to the client. I also keep copies of all other files, including correspondence, html files, and graphic files, within the client's folder. If you adopt this method of organization, it means that you'll always know where to start looking for a file.

Create a method of naming files that works for you. Windows 95 allows you to use long (up to 256 character) file names, but a lot of older Windows programs won't recognize the file's full name and will truncate it, thus **Big_Header_Number_One.tif** becomes **Big_Hea~.tif**.

2 Use a file management utility like Thumbs Plus (as shown in Figure 11.9) or Corel's Multimedia Manager to keep visual checks on your files. With either of these two utilities, you can rename, move, or delete files. Can't remember if goofy1.gif is the final art or goofy3.gif?

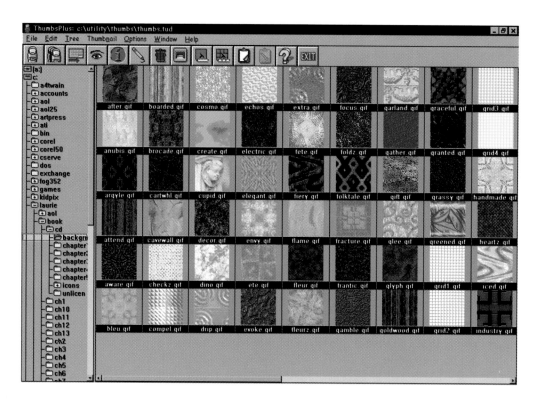

Figure 11.9 Thumbsplus file utility

ThumbsPlus is shareware, available on CompuServe and AOL. You can check the Resources section at the back of the book for more information. If you're working in Corel PhotoPaint and want to use the Multimedia Manager, you can use the application launcher icon on the toolbar you worked on earlier in this chapter (see Figure 11.10).

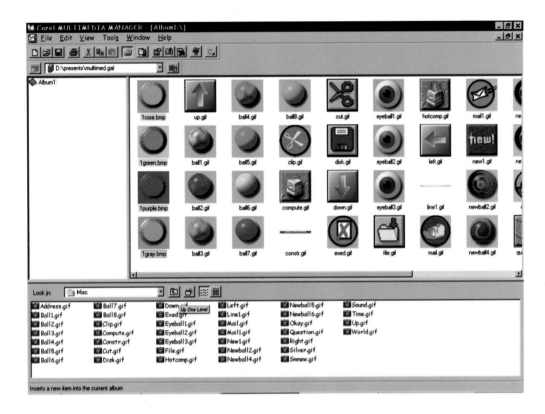

Figure 11.10 Corel's MultiMedia Manager

3 Can't find a file? Afraid that it's lost and gone forever? Try using the Find function off of the **Start** button from within Windows.

4 Run a lean, clean machine. Get rid of unnecessary files, empty the Recycle Bin, and use the Windows disk utilities ScanDisk and Defrag after you've moved or deleted a lot of files. Photoshop, and many other software applications use contiguous hard disk space for part of its swap space when you're working on files. Using Defrag will move files to leave more contiguous free space on your disk. I run Defrag about once a week.

5 Save the original, 24-bit RGB uncompressed versions of your files. Why? Because there are two new graphics formats on the horizon: interlaced jpg and Johnson Grace's .ART file format. And that's just this week. Standards for the web, whether they are graphics, html, viewers or browsers change constantly. To convert to either of these newer file formats, you would get the best result by starting with the original uncompressed files.

To find out more about the jpg format, you can read the JPEG FAQ at http://www.cis.ohio-state.edu/hypertext/faq/usente/jpeg-faq/faq.html. To find out more about the art file format, you can visit the Johnson Grace website at http://www.jgc.com/

6 Clean out your web browser's cache. When you view web pages from a web browser, the files are stored on your hard disk in a directory named Cache. The reason the files are stored in cache is to speed up viewing the graphics at a website. If you use the back icon after you've looked at a website, the browser will reload the html and graphics files for that website from your cache. Loading from cache is much quicker than loading files from the website. Most browsers allow you to set a maximum size for the Cache directory. The Cache directory can get filled up pretty quickly, and it not only takes up precious hard disk space, it can give you misleading information.

To give an example, I recently went to check some changes I had done at my website. I was amazed to find that none of the new graphics were showing up. The mystery was cleared up when I realized that the browser was reading the older graphics file stored on my computer in cache, and wasn't reading from the website at all. Using the **Reload** button will force the browser to reference the files at the website, and not the files in cache.

For most browsers, you can set the way you view graphics by selecting **Preferences** or **Options** from the menu bar. Under Netscape, for example, you can select **Options/Preferences/Cache & Network/Verify Documents**. The next choice you make (Once Per Session/Every Time/Never) determines when the browser will reload the page from the website. Also within this same dialog box you'll see the "**Clear Disk Cache Now**" button. This is how you would clear all the older files stored in the browser's cache off of your computer.

If you use several browsers on your computer in order to check the appearance of web pages and graphics, the amount of disk space that is tied up in cache can be considerable.

7 Back up your hard disk. Oh, I know you've heard it before. But I had a six-month-old, nearly full 1.08-gig drive fail without warning recently, so I thought I would remind you.

CHAPTER 12

YOUR FAVORITE CARTOON CHARACTER HAS A VERY GOOD LAWYER

I can't think of a single field that has expanded as quickly as the web. Everyone keeps waiting for the growth and interest in the WWW to peak, and it hasn't yet.

Sometimes, acquiring knowledge becomes secondary to getting the website up. Recently, in an online forum, a web designer was asking for some feedback on a new website. I looked over to the website, which was (ironically enough,) for a public relations firm that specialized in disaster management. Very prominently displayed in the main web page was a very familiar (and very much copyrighted) cartoon character.

The day after I sent an e-mail to the designer of the website, letting her know about the copyrighted work on the web page, the cartoon was gone.

There are two areas of copyright to be aware of: (1) using work that is not your own, and (2) the copyright of your artwork.

There are many untested legal areas of the web, but ownership of artwork is not one of them. What you create belongs to you, unless you specifically say that you're allowing others to use it. This is an especially sticky problem area on the web because of the right mouse button.

THE RIGHT MOUSE BUTTON

By depressing the right mouse button from within many browsers, you have a very simple way to download the artwork. Even if a browser doesn't support this function, getting a screen capture is not brain surgery. You should be aware that it is very easy for someone to steal the work you've done. It's the equivalent of keeping your portfolio in an unlocked room.

Netscape (Figure 12.1) and America Online's browser (Figure 12.2) are two of the most popular browsers in use at the moment. Using the right button on either of these browsers allows you to save the image directly to your hard disk.

Figure 12.1 The right mouse button used in Netscape

Figure 12.2 The right mouse button used in AOL's browser

In a sense, I think we're back to philosophy and the web. You can become so paranoid about theft that you never put anything up on your website. You can certainly choose not to put up artwork that you don't want stolen, and take a blood oath to track down to the ends of the earth anyone who uses your artwork without permission.

The Internet has a history of free exchange of information, and some users may not realize that ownership of artwork is even an issue. Artwork taken from a website and used elsewhere without permission is done much more frequently out of ignorance than malice. A simple letter to someone who is displaying your artwork without permission informing them of the ownership of the artwork is often sufficient to educate the misuser and convince him or her to take the work off their website. Additionally, placing a notice about copyright or ownership of artwork on your website may also convince someone to think twice about using artwork you have created.

In any case, you should definitely become more familiar with copyright. There are two FAQs of interest. One is the general copyright FAQ, at http://www.cis.ohio-state.edu/hypertext/faq/usenet/Copyright-FAQ/top.html, and the other is the Copyright Myths FAQ, available at http://www.clari.net/brad/Copymyths.html/.

STOP! DON'T USE THAT CLIPART ON YOUR WEB PAGE!

If you've read the licensing agreement for the clipart that you have (and I know you have), you will recall a little paragraph about not allowing electronic distribution of the clipart. You can't really get any closer to electronic distribution than posting something to a web page.

For instance, the Corel Guidelines for Clipart Use, found at the front of the CorelDRAW 6 clipart book, says "You may not...use the clipart images' electronic format...unless the clipart image is embedded and for viewing purposes only."

I've been checking with various clipart companies, and there is no one single answer for using clipart on web pages. Many companies hadn't come up with a decision about clipart and Web use at the time I asked.

Corel's decision is that you can use their clipart on a Web page, as long as the clipart is used for decoration on the page, and isn't the reason for the Web page. That decision only applies to the Corel clipart—the Corel collection of clipart actually includes artwork from seven other companies.

You can check who owns a particular piece of clipart by opening the clipart within the Corel Multimedia Manager, and using the right mouse button to select **Properties**. You can see in the **Keyword** box who owns the clipart. In Figure 12.3, you can see that Image Club is the owner.

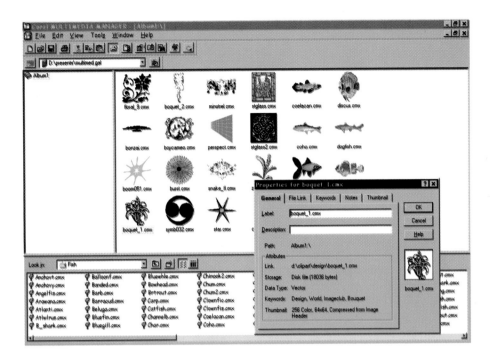

Figure 12.3 Using the Corel MultiMedia Manager to find the clipart's creator

You should check with the creator of the clipart you are using before you use it on your website.

APPENDIX A: RESOURCES

This appendix references valuable Internet resources for software companies, and newsgroups that help you when creating web graphics. Now that most software companies have their own websites, it's easy to download updates and patches for your programs. Typically, newsgroups offer the most recent news on using software, what's happening in HTML, and new web standards.

SOFTWARE RESOURCES

Adobe Photoshop

Adobe Photoshop is the acknowledged standard for image manipulation. There is an Adobe forum on CompuServe (**GO ADOBEAPP**), and a Photoshop discussion area on America Online (Keyword: **adobe**). You can find updates for Photoshop at their website.

Adobe Systems Incorporated
1585 Charleston Road
PO Box 7900
Mountain View, CA 94039-7900
(800) 521-1976
http://www.adobe.com/

ART File Format

Johnson Grace has developed an image compression file format named art. You can find out more about it at their website.

Johnson Grace
http://www.jgc.com/

The Black Box Filters

Alien Skin Software
322 Chapanoke, Suite 101
Raleigh, NC 27603
(919) 662-4934
AlienSkin@aol.com

Alien Skin makes a set of filters called the Black Box that are useful for creating drop shadows, beveled edges, and so on.

Corel PhotoPaint 6.0

Corel PhotoPaint 6.0 is sold as a stand-alone product and is also bundled in with CorelDRAW.

There is a Corel forum on CompuServe (**GO CORELAPP**), and a Corel Message Board **n** on America Online (Keyword: **corel**).

Corel Corporation

The Corel Building

1600 Carling Avenue

Ottawa, Ontario

Canada K1Z 8R7

(613) 728-8200

GIF Construction Set

GIF Construction Set for Windows will allow you to create transparent gifs. It also supports interlacing. GIF Construction Set is available on AOL, CompuServe, and:

```
ftp.uunorth.north.net:
/pub/alchemy
```

Alchemy Mindworks Inc.

PO Box 500

Beeton, Ontario

Canada LOG 1A0

(800) 263-1138

70451.2734@CompuServe.com

GifTrans

GifTrans is a DOS command-line program to create transparent gifs.

It is available from:

```
ftp.rz.uni-karlsruhe.de/
pub/net/www/tools/
giftrans.exe
```

Image Alchemy

Image Alchemy is a DOS program for converting between different image file formats. Handmade Software also makes a UNIX version of Image Alchemy. You can download a demo of Image Alchemy from their website.

Handmade Software

48820 Kato Road, Suite 100

Fremont, CA 94538

(510) 252-0101

(800) 252-0101

info@handmadesw.com

http://www.handmadesw.com/

Image Club Graphics

Image Club sells a variety of fonts, clip art, filters, photo clip art, and so forth.

You can browse their website for more information on products and pricing.

Image Club Graphics
10545 West Donges Court
Milwaukee, WI 53224-9967
Orders (800) 661-9410
Catalog Requests (800) 387-9193
http://www.adobe.com/imageclub/

JPEG FAQ

The JPEG FAQ is available at:

```
http://www.cis.ohio-state.edu/
hypertext/faq/usenet/jpeg-faq/
faq.html
```

LView Pro

There are five versions of LView Pro. Find a copy of version 1.C (32-bit) or later.

LView Pro is available on CompuServe, AOL, and from the following sites:

http://world.std.com/~mmedia/
http://mirror.wwa.com/mirror/busdir/lview/lview.html
ftp.www.acs.oakland.edu/oak/SimTel/win3/graphics/lviewp1b.zip

Mmedia Research
Attn.: Leonardo Haddad Loureiro
1501 E. Hallandale Beach Blvd., #254
Hallandale, FL 33009

Paint Shop Pro 3.11

Version 3.1 creates transparent and interlaced gifs. This is also a very nice shareware paint package with many capabilities you would expect only from higher end commercial paint packages. The only drawback to using Paint Shop Pro to create transparent gifs is that you can't preview the area of your gif that is being made transparent.

JASC has a forum on CompuServe at **GO WINAPC**. Paint Shop Pro version 3.1 is available on CompuServe, AOL, and ftp:

```
ftp.winternet.com/users/
jasc/psp301.zip
```

```
ftp.www.acs.oakland.edu/
oak/SimTel/win3/graphics/
psp301.zip
```

JASC
PO Box 44997
Eden Prairie, MN 55344
(800)622-2793
http://www.winternet.com/~jasc/

PhotoGif

PhotoGif is available from the following sites:

http://aris.com/boxtop

BoxTop Software
PO Box 2347
Starkville, MS 39760-2347
(601) 324-7352
email: boxtop@aris.com

PhotoGif is a shareware plug-in filter created by BoxTop Software that will work with any paint program that supports Photoshop-compatible plug-ins. There is also a Mac version of PhotoGif.

Thumbs Plus

Thumbs Plus is a file manager, especially helpful in dealing with graphics files.

Cerious Software
1515 Mockingbird Lane Suite 803
Charlotte, NC 28209
(704) 529-0200
cerious@vnet.net

NEWSGROUPS

alt.corel.graphics

alt.fractal.design.painter

alt.soft-sys.corel.draw

comp.fonts

comp.graphics.apps.photoshop

comp.infosystems.www.authoring.html

comp.infosystems.www.authoring.images

comp.infosystems.www.authoring.misc

WEBSITES

Photoshop Websites

http://inorganic.chem.ufl.edu/alf/photos.htm
Information on Photoshop and links to other Photoshop websites

http://www.winternet.com/~faz/pshop/index.html
More information on Photoshop.

CorelDRAW Website

CorelNet
http://www.corelnet.com/

Appendix B

HTML Tags for Graphics

HTML is a standard for creating web pages out of ordinary and easily transferable text files. The text is formatted and graphics are added by the use of tags, which are like small commands placed between the less-than and greater-than characters. <B>, for instance, is the tag for bold. There are only a few tags for graphics, and all of them are fairly simple. These tags are all taken from the HTML 3.0 specification, which is slowly reaching stability. The main tag you'll be using for graphics is IMG, though the BACKGROUND tags are good for defining your pages' overall look.

IMG

The IMG tag lets you drop images into your text wherever you like. In its most basic form, you'll be using it with just a file name and (hopefully) some alternative text in case your readers aren't downloading images. A simple tag might read:

```
<IMG SRC="sample.gif" ALT="This is a sample picture.">
```

If the user was using a text-only browser or had turned off downloading images, the text "This is a sample picture." would appear on the page. Otherwise the image sample.gif would appear, because the SRC="" section indicates where the browser should get the graphic. Although you don't have to include alternative text, it's a good idea, especially if the image gets used for a hyperlink.

Other attributes can be included in this tag. For instance, you can specify the height and width of the picture in pixels, which makes it easier (and faster!) for a browser to lay out the text for a page while the graphics are still downloading. If your image was 72 pixels tall and 360 pixels wide, you'd add height and width to the tag as follows:

```
<IMG SRC="sample.gif" HEIGHT=72 WIDTH=360 ALT="This is a
sample picture.">
```

Another popular tag for graphics is the ALIGN tag. Originally this just took the values TOP, MIDDLE, and BOTTOM, specifying how a graphic should fit with a line of text. LEFT and RIGHT were early additions to the specification, allowing designers to put a graphic on the left or right margin of a page and have text wrap along the edges. If you wanted to align the sample picture on the right margin, you'd add the alignment to the tag like this:

```
<IMG SRC="sample.gif" HEIGHT=72 WIDTH=360 ALIGN=RIGHT
ALT="This is a sample picture.">
```

The last tag that gets a lot of use is the ISMAP tag, which tells the browser to return the coordinates of where the user clicked on the graphics to the server. This only works if you made the image a link to a program that can respond to the coordinates, like this:

```
<A HREF="http://www.com/cgi-bin/samplemap"><IMG
SRC="sample.gif" ISMAP></A>
```

When the user clicks on the picture, the server will get a message saying what part of the map received a click, allowing you to create interactive imagemaps.

Backgrounds

Backgrounds get defined in the HTML body tag. In the old days, the BODY tag just said <BODY> at the top of the main text of your page. Now the BODY tag includes lots of extra information about what your page looks like. Backgrounds are covered in Chapter 4, and go behind the rest of your page. To specify them, you would include the BACKGROUND tag in the BODY tag like this:

```
<BODY BACKGROUND="background.gif">
```

You can also include the BGCOLOR, TEXT, LINK, and VLINK tags, which specify in hex (see Chapter 5) the colors you want used for background color, the main text, links, and links your reader has already visited. It's not always a great idea to change these, but it can help keep text from disappearing into your backgrounds.

For more on the HTML 3.0 specifications, including tags for text, pay a visit to http://www.w3.org/hypertext/WWW/MarkUp/html3/

GLOSSARY

Browser
The software (such as Mosaic, Netscape, Internet Explorer) that allows you to view the World Wide Web.

EPS
Encapsulated Post Script format. A vector-based file format that includes a low-resolution graphic used for placement and a Post Script file that allows you to print at high resolution.

GIF
Graphics Interchange Format. A compressed image file format. A gif image is always composed of 256 colors or less.

Header
An image at the top of a web page. Usually the main graphic for a website.

HTML
Hyper Text Mark-Up Language, used to create web pages.

Icon
A small graphic image, sometimes called a button, that is used to navigate software or a website.

Indexed color image
An image whose colors are constrained to a specific number of colors. In the case of GIF files, the number of colors are constrained (or indexed) to 256 or less.

Interlacing
An interlaced graphic will load in a number of stages to a web browser. Each stage displays a higher resolution version of the image.

JPEG
A 24-bit, lossy compression file format for web graphics. JPEG allows you to choose the quality of graphic. The lower the quality, the smaller the JPEG file will be.

Lossless
A compression method where no information is lost during compression. Using WinZip or PKZip to compress a file or group of files, for example, is a lossless way to compress a file. Once unzipped, all of the original information in the file is still available. Unfortunately, zipped graphics won't display in a web page.

Lossy

Refers to a compression method where information from the original graphic is lost during compression. JPEG and GIF are both lossy formats, which is a good reason to always keep a copy of the original file.

Noninterlaced

A graphic that loads in a single pass from top to bottom.

Pixel

The smallest unit of a computer-graphic image.

Screenshot or **Screen capture**

A picture of a computer screen, usually used to demonstrate the features of software. To create a simple screenshot in Windows, use the **Print Screen** key on the keyboard, and then open a paint program and use the **Paste** command to paste the screen shot from the Windows clipboard into an image.

Thumbnail

A smaller version of a larger file. In traditional graphic arts, ideas are usually sketched out first in a small (thumbnail) format. On the Web, thumbnails are used to conserve space. Thumbnails are usually linked to the larger versions of a file, downloaded only when a reader doesn't mind the wait.

Transparency

A single color of a GIF image may be assigned transparency, so that the background color of the Web page will show through.

URL

Universal Resource Locator, the format for web addresses. For example, the URL for the category Computer Artwork on the search directory Yahoo is:

```
http://www.yahoo.com/Arts/Computer_Generated/
```

Visit the Web Diner on America Online

When stopping by the Web Diner on America Online, you can take a free HTML class, pick up some graphics tips, and download a new daily graphic, too! This forum (which I developed with three online colleagues) is devoted to helping small businesses put their websites up on AOL.

The Web Diner offers HTML classes twice a week. In thirty minutes, AOL members write their first HTML page and put it up on the AOL server. At the end of class, everyone can see their first web page live on the web!

The two daily changing specials at the Web Diner are:

The Web Diner
keyword: Diner

- the Blue Plate Special, a recommended website.

- the Byte of the Day, a heaping helping of HTML, graphics, or other helpful web tips.

Interested in what other AOL members are doing on the web? Check out Family Recipes, where the Web Diner is offering free links to AOL member websites.

On America Online, use keyword: **Diner**

The FREE ART Website

If you have enjoyed the graphics and tips in this book, you should visit my FREE ART Website at http://www.mccannas.com, and discover even more Photoshop and PhotoPaint tips and techniques. Learn how to set your type on fire and emboss a graphic. You can download icons, seamless background tiles and examples created in this book.

http://www.mccannas.com